Y0-BRE-572

# WILDLIFE '78

Published in collaboration with the World Wildlife Fund

# WILDLIFE '78
## The World Conservation Yearbook
## Edited by Nigel Sitwell

The Danbury Press

Previous page: a caribou in
Mount McKinley National
Park, Alaska. The proposed
addition of land on the north
side of the park would add
critical habitat for the caribou,
as well as for the moose and
wolves

First published in the United States of America in 1978
by The Danbury Press, a division of
Grolier Enterprises Inc.
Publisher: Robert B. Clarke

ISBN: 0 7172 8120 5
Library of Congress Catalog Card Number: 77 17663

© London Editions and
World Wildlife Fund International 1978

*All rights reserved*
No part of this publication may be reproduced, stored in
a retrieval system, or transmitted in any form or by any
means, electronic, mechanical, photographic or otherwise
without the prior permission of the copyright owner.

This book has been designed and produced by
London Editions Ltd.,
30 Uxbridge Road, London W12 8ND

Printed in Spain by Printer industria gráfica sa
Sant Vicenç dels Horts   Barcelona 1978
Depósito Legal B. 16337-1978

While it is intended that the information and opinions
expressed in this book reflect the policies of the World
Wildlife Fund and its sister organization, the
International Union for Conservation of Nature and
Natural Resources, the contents are the responsibility of
the various contributors and the editor.

## Contributors

**Sir Peter Scott CBE DSC** Chairman, World Wildlife Fund

**Nigel Sitwell** Advisory Panel, World Wildlife Fund Britain
**William Oliver** Jersey Wildlife Preservation Trust
**Keith Laidler** Survival Anglia
**Dr Iain Douglas-Hamilton** Elephant Group, IUCN
**Dr Norman Myers** Consultant in Environmental Conservation
**Erich Hoyt**
**David McKelvey** ICBP
**Malcolm Penny** Survival Anglia
**Dr Anne LaBastille**
**Dr Bryan Nelson** University of Aberdeen
**Romulus and Zahida Whitaker** Madras Snake Park
**David Black** World Wildlife Fund Britain
**Leigh Plester** Helsinki University
**Erwin A. Bauer**
**Bryan Sage** Ecologist, British Petroleum
**John A. Burton** Assistant Secretary, Fauna Preservation Society
**Michael Gore**

# CONTENTS

# FOREWORD

Sir Peter Scott

This book highlights a number of wildlife conservation problems in various parts of the world. Some of the stories are positive and encouraging, while others describe problems that may be hard to solve. We should all like to conserve as much as possible of what still remains of the natural world, and as many of the species of wild animals and plants as we can. We want to do this because we believe that mankind needs wildlife, needs contact with wild nature, in order to lead a fulfilled and satisfying life. But we also believe that there are very strong scientific reasons for conserving nature. We feel, for example, that it is essential to preserve as much as possible of the genetic diversity represented by all the different kinds of plants and animals which currently share our planet with us.

But we are constantly aware that we have to make our case for conservation to people who may not be as lucky as we are. It is one thing for me, living in a relatively prosperous part of the developed world, to understand the intellectual justification for wildlife conservation. Some might say it is a luxury I can afford to indulge. But there are other people in the world less fortunate to whom conservation is either an abstract concept with no bearing on their day-to-day lives, or a nuisance to which they merely pay lip service.

If we believe, as I do, that conservation of the natural environment is important not only for its own sake, but for the very survival of the human race, then we have to somehow convince all people that its long-term significance outweighs the short-term gains they may make from over-exploiting renewable natural resources today. There are several articles in this book which illustrate this conflict, notably John Burton's account of the exploitation of Phuket Island's marine resources, the Whitakers' article about snakes, and the discussion of how man and pygmy hog both use the same thatch forest habitat in north-eastern India.

Conservation of the world's wildlife and wild places will only succeed, in the long run, if the people on the spot become convinced that it is in their own best interests. That is the scale of the challenge.

*Slimbridge*
*September 1977*

# INTRODUCTION

## by Nigel Sitwell

Nigel Sitwell in the Aguada
Blanca reserve, home of
vicuña, flamingoes, and other
waterbirds, in the Peruvian
Andes

Not long ago newspapers around the world headlined the hunting of two very rare species of animals, the spectacled bear and the huemul, —in fact, only one, the huemul, was actually shot, although licenses were issued for both— by a wealthy and famous sportsman. Part of the trouble was caused by the fact that the ordinary people in the country concerned are not normally allowed to hunt these animals, and it appeared that there was one game law for the poor and another for the rich foreigner. The upshot of the affair was beneficial, however, as it probably encouraged the country concerned, and other countries as well, to enforce their game laws with greater determination.

But although it was understandable that conservationists should attack this particular hunting incident, and make an example of it, the fact is that sport hunting is a somewhat insignificant threat to wildlife in most parts of the world. A greater problem is illegal hunting, or poaching, either for the pot or for some other material gain by people who often need to do it to survive. By its nature this kind of hunting is uncontrolled, and takes a far greater toll of wildlife than sport hunting. It is also harder to deal with because one knows that the hunters tend to have few alternative sources of food, or income.

The articles in this book on the elephant and the leopard illustrate this kind of problem, though in these cases the animals are poached for the value of their tusks and skins rather than (primarily) for their meat. If there were not a flourishing demand for ivory and leopard skin in the developed countries, there would probably be far less poaching than there is. Ultimately, this kind of wildlife exploitation can only be controlled effectively by controlling the trade.

Nevertheless, the trade in wildlife products and the poaching that takes place to meet the demand, is a far less important factor in the disappearance of wildlife species than encroachment on or destruction of their habitat. All over the world burgeoning human numbers result in one way or another in the gradual removal or despoilment of wilderness habitats. Several articles illustrate this theme all too clearly. The pygmy hog is even now only surviving in isolated islands of its preferred habitat, the thatchlands of Assam. Its only hope, in fact, is that some of these areas can be maintained in a pristine state, despite their economic importance for the local people. Two birds, Abbott's booby and the Mauritius kestrel, live on islands and only continue to survive because some of their habitat still remains. In general, wildlife conservation becomes habitat conservation. Give an animal species a large enough place to live and it will probably survive.

For this reason, national parks and nature reserves have become a cornerstone of wildlife conservation policy. Some countries are relatively rich in space and can afford to declare large areas as protected. McKinley is in Alaska which is lucky enough to have plenty of space and so the establishment or enlargement of protected areas there is still relatively easy. Abuko is in a very small country—The Gambia —but one where the development of a sound conservation policy is understood at the topmost levels. In fact, many of the less developed countries in various parts of the world are doing better than the rich and developed nations in setting aside areas for national parks and other protected areas.

Effective conservation very often requires a change in traditional attitudes towards animals. Who would have imagined that saving ants from destruction would provide direct benefits for man? And yet they are a vital part of many food chains and once it is pointed out how important they are it is easy to understand why they deserve to be protected and nurtured. It is good, too, that European children are being encouraged to play a leading role in saving the wood ants' nests. Having become involved in such a project during childhood, it is likely that the adult will tend to take the 'conservationist' line and grow up with an attitude towards our fellow creatures that is much more sympathetic that it would have been otherwise.

Another group of insects that have a re-

latively hard time in the twentieth century is the butterflies. But they are seldom persecuted directly. Either it is removal of a suitable food supply which threatens them—or, as with the northern butterflies of Finland, it is the threat to their boggy habitats. Bogs are like marshes and mangrove swamps: few people besides biologists recognize the tremendous importance of some of these superficially useless places. The destruction of mangrove swamps is probably one of the most senseless acts, as so much of the marine life we enjoy and need to eat starts life there; it is incredibly short-sighted to exploit the mangroves for fuel, or because they can be reclaimed, perhaps as a site for a holiday hotel. It is to be hoped that the Thai Government will appreciate what is happening to Phuket Island in time (and not only to the mangrove swamps).

The marine environment is something of a paradox for conservationists. On the one hand, as far as the general public is concerned, the world's seas and oceans seem to be vast—a vast and inexhaustible resource, where fish and many other good things to eat are caught, and also a vast dumping ground; it seems inconceivable to many people that the seas could ever 'run out of' fish, or could ever cease to be a continuing receptacle for as much rubbish (of all sorts) as we care to pour into it. On the other hand, as conservationists, fishermen, and others are rapidly coming to realize, the marine environment is seriously threatened. Our last great resource, as it has been called, is in danger of being destroyed.

Several small, more or less enclosed seas, like the Baltic, are practically 'dead seas' due to the amount of toxic effluent that has been poured into them. Others, like the Mediterranean, are no longer quite the holiday paradises they once were: beach after beach all around the Mediterranean is so grossly polluted that on occasion the authorities have to forbid bathing.

The sea's products are being steadily over-exploited. Tropical islands and their surrounding reefs seem particularly vulnerable to the pressures generated by a thriving tourist industry. The largest of all mammals—the whales—have all but vanished due to man's greed. Many fisheries are in trouble following thoughtless over-harvesting in the past: mackerel and cod are familiar examples. And by the time you read this a conference will have taken place on the Antarctic Treaty—which may have opened the door to the sticky hands of a score of countries plundering the rich waters of the Southern Ocean (as well as digging into the Antarctic Continent itself for minerals). Antarctica has been the one outstanding example of a major ecosystem that mankind has managed, by mutual agreement between nations, to avoid spoiling. It should of course be allowed to remain unspoiled, but the pessimists believe the writing is already on the wall for Antarctica.

The World Wildlife Fund in association with the International Union for Conservation of Nature launched a $10 million campaign at the end of 1976 called 'The Seas Must Live'. The campaign was divided into a series of large and small projects dealing with particular species or groups of species, and critically threatened habitats, in the world's marine environment. The global commons represented by the oceans should be conserved by governments, for no non-governmental organization can possibly have the financial resources or power to control human activity on the necessary scale. But in the absence of clear signs that such governmental will-power is developing, the WWF/IUCN campaign is a vitally important beginning of concern. May it be a catalyst, rather than an end in itself.

But to return to the national park/nature reserve context, Dr Ian McTaggart of the University of British Columbia has said that he regards the 'park idea' as 'one of the great inventions of the twentieth century . . . Parks are more and more becoming islands surrounded by a sea of man-altered landscape. One of the major roles of national parks around the world is to maintain the rich diversity with which this world is endowed.' So the parks are becoming rather like museums of natural history—living museums to be sure, but museums all the same. If this seems depressing, let us contemplate how much more depressing life would be without them! And so long as we do maintain these living museums, with their rich diversity of genetic material, both plant and animal, it is always possible that with the advent of some better world in the future, we may be able to draw on these banks. And they are worth maintaining just because of their insurance role. Our grandchildren may be grateful to us for our foresight.

# MAMMALS

## SURVIVAL UNCERTAIN FOR THE PYGMY HOG

William Oliver

The recent history of the pygmy hog has become a saga of success and failure. This was a species that some people, quite unjustifiably, had considered to have become extinct, probably in the early 1960s. Their reasons for this assumption were simply that no recent reports about sightings, captures, or killings had filtered through to the local authorities for some years. In 1964, E. P. Gee wisely left the question open when he wrote in his book, *The Wildlife of India*, that he feared 'this species may have become extinct or nearly so'. Moreover, he actively sought information about it and encouraged others to do likewise. These others included some British tea planters in north-west Assam where the species was formerly known to have occurred. With the interest in the species that was stimulated in this way, it was not long before rumors of its continued existence along the Assam–Bhutan international border began to percolate through to these interested people. One of the latter was Gerald Durrell, author and founder of the Jersey Wildlife Preservation Trust, who proposed that an expedition should be mounted to search for the animal.

However, this proposal was overtaken by events, for in March 1971 one of the tea plantation managers, Richard Graves, actually acquired some live pygmy hogs simply by purchasing them from plantation workers and local villagers who were selling them at the weekly bazaar. It was later found that these people had been catching *nul gowri* (grass pig) for years during the dry season for local consumption.

The pygmy hog was first recorded in 1847 and was described by B. H. Hodgson in his paper 'On a new form of Hog Kind or Suidae', in the *Journal of the Field Society*. Hodgson stated that it must seem almost incredible that so tiny an animal should effectively resist men, but considered that the pygmy hog escaped notice owing to its being exclusively confined to the deep recesses of primeval forest. There have been relatively few documented accounts of the species since that time, but this was not altogether surprising in view of the hog's small size, its secretive habits, the very dense nature of its preferred thatchland habitat, and its somewhat (scientifically) remote distribution.

The pygmy hogs acquired by Graves had actually been caught on the Attreekhat Tea Estate in the Mangaldai area of northern Assam. It appeared that the hogs had sought refuge in the tea garden because of an extensive fire in the thatch-scrub jungle to the north of the plantation. The remuneration that was offered for the acquisition of these animals encouraged further captures and a total of seventeen animals were obtained in this way during March and April 1971. All these were at first accommodated at the Attreekhat Tea Estate, but some were also sent to the nearby Paneery and Budlapara Tea Estates soon afterwards, to minimize the consequences of any virulent infection. Several of these animals had severe leg injuries, having been caught in gin traps, and one male and two females died within a short time.

Whilst Durrell's proposed expedition was made unnecessary by these events, Jeremy

**The present status of the pygmy hog is one of the ironies of wildlife conservation. Though 'reprieved' from extinction by its rediscovery in 1971, it is again (or still) in serious danger of vanishing altogether**

Mallinson was requested to go to Assam on his behalf, under the sponsorship of the Fauna Preservation society, to advise on general husbandry and conservation policy. The re-appearance of the pygmy hog had led Richard Magor, director of the tea company concerned, to found the Assam Valley Wildlife Society to raise money for the conservation of these and other animals in Assam, and funds were to be set aside for pygmy hog projects.

The color of the pygmy hogs was blackish-brown, shaded with ginger, the hairs being quite sparsely distributed over the body compared with those of a wild boar. Both ears and the tail were short and without hair, and the shoulder height of the largest male was no more than eleven inches and its weight about eight kilograms. They moved around their improvised run, a converted chicken house, in fits and starts, but when disturbed from their bedding of thatch they were able to move like lightning, keeping close together, the females usually following the males, before reaching another refuge where they would pile pyramid-fashion on top of each other.

In 1847 Hodgson said that the pygmy hog seems to have the disposition of the peccary. He added that the males will fearlessly attack intruders, charging and cutting the naked legs of their human or other attackers with a speed that baffles the eye. Writing in 1921, Frederic Lord Hamilton described a shooting expedition with the Maharajah of Cooch Bihar in 1891. He stated that the hogs went about in droves of about fifty, and moved through the grass with such incredible speed that the eye was unable to follow them. The elephants, oddly enough, were apparently scared of the pygmy hogs, 'for the little creatures have tusks as sharp as razors, and gash the elephants' feet with them as they rush past.'

One is forced to wonder, however, about the circumstances that elicited this sort of behavior, for the pygmy hogs handled by Jeremy Mallinson in 1971 were surprisingly non-aggressive and from all accounts no real aggression was encountered even when they were caught. On the contrary, they proved to be extremely nervous and great caution had to be shown until the animals had settled down as they tend to panic and run blind and may sustain damage by collision with perimeter fences or other structures in their enclosures. However, like so many timorous animals with an extreme

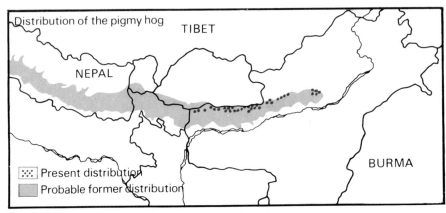

Distribution of the pigmy hog

TIBET · NEPAL · BURMA

▨ Present distribution
▧ Probable former distribution

tendency to flight, once they have established a safe zone within a known territory, they may become very tame. Richard Magor noted that certain animals will even appear to welcome and enjoy human company, coming out of cover to greet people whom they know, often relishing attention and even rolling over to be scratched on their stomachs.

The animals proved to be essentially diurnal, being active from shortly after dawn to well after dusk, with an inactive phase during the hot midday. They build substantial communal nests, that are constructed co-operatively by both males and females. These nests are comprised of large quantities of thatch or other long grasses that are piled over a pit dug into the ground with their snouts. This depression is shallow, but the earth is pushed outwards so that a rim is formed above ground level. The pigs therefore lie slightly below ground level with the thatch canopy protecting them from the elements. This construction is very effective as the nests are lined and are dry and warm inside, though prolonged rain necessitates new nest construction quite regularly. It is often difficult to tell whether a nest is occupied or not and it is possible to walk right up to a pygmy hog nest before they will break cover. There is a main exit and entrance hole but this is often difficult to find for the thatch falls back into place very easily.

Several litters of pygmy hogs have been born in captivity in Assam in recent years. Litter sizes have varied from three to six and all of the births have occurred in the two months of April and May. In Assam this coincides with the pre-monsoon showers known as 'the little rains' (or *chota* rains) that fall mostly in April and have the effect of resuscitating the vegetation. The main monsoons are in June and though the jungle and thatchlands of the

**The pygmy hog has never been much studied by zoologists, probably because of its small size and secretive habits. It stands no more than eleven inches (less than thirty centimeters) at the shoulder, and lives in the dense thatch-scrub forest of north-western Assam in India**

Himalayan foothill habitat of the pygmy hog are not usually seriously waterlogged, the newly born piglets benefit from the additional food supplies which become available with the revival of the grasslands after the chota rains; they are well developed by the time the main monsoons arrive.

As part of the captive breeding program, it was agreed that the Jersey Wildlife Preservation Trust could export up to four pygmy hogs to Europe. Accordingly, Jeremy Mallinson went to Assam again in November 1976 to bring back a proven breeding pair. These animals, which were loaned by the Assam authorities, were taken to Zurich Zoo in Switzerland as part of a cooperative agreement, because direct importation into the UK was precluded by quarantine regulations. A litter of five piglets was born in Zurich on 1 May 1977, the first in Europe since London Zoo bred them in 1886.

However, despite the successful breeding of several litters in Assam and the long-term maintenance of a few individuals, the captive breeding projects have not been a success and the captive animals in Assam have only been maintained by the acquisition of fresh animals every year. Since 1971 at least forty animals have been caught, always in March, April, and May following dry season burning. Mortality has remained unjustifiably high owing to crude methods of capture, the flighty disposition of the animals themselves, and poor management of the captive animals. The potential from such large number of acquisitions is obviously great, yet there are only a handful of animals now in captivity in Assam, in the State Zoo at Gauhati and on one of the tea estates. In fairness, however, it must be said that although this effort has been unsuccessful in its primary objective of boosting the population of these animals, much has been learnt about their behavior and reproductive biology. Perhaps more important still, they have created considerable public and official interest in the species—though this interest has yet to be realized in terms of any real action towards stemming the decline of wild populations by the creation of reserves or sanctuaries for protection of the species.

Moreover, captive breeding is not a solution to the endangered species problem even if it is successful, and the continued research and breeding must go hand in hand with efforts to reverse current trends in the wild. But very little was known about the situation in the wild and a better understanding of that was clearly a prerequisite for a meaningful conservation policy. Accordingly, on behalf of the Jersey Trust, I visited India in March 1977 for a three-month field survey sponsored by the Assam Valley Wildlife Society and the Jersey Wildlife Preservation Trust.

The habitat of the pygmy hog is best described as 'thatch-scrub jungle'—the typical high-grass, thinly forested upland savanna of the Himalayan foothills. The thatch, or elephant grass, grows to a height of about four meters during the monsoons which last from June to October, but withers down to about two meters during the dry season from October until March. This sort of habitat is interspersed with belts of mixed deciduous and evergreen primary forest and is now found only in sanctuaries and forest reserves: since it is well drained, it is ideal for conversion to settlement and agriculture. It is probable that the pygmy hog once occurred widely over the northern sub-continent of India, and it has been recorded from Nepal, through Sikkim, North Bengal, and parts of southern Bhutan to north-western Assam, though nearly all post-1971 records have been confined to the latter areas. An American expedition from the Hormel Institute failed to find the species in Nepal in 1964 and it is likely that it is now confined entirely to this part of north-western Assam.

However, there is comparatively little 'wilderness' left in Assam owing to the continuous and progressive settlement and cultivation of an expanding and immigrating people. Land is under tremendous pressure and the rate of transformation of the former habitat has been dramatic in the past few decades. This is a continuing process and the human population increase has been accelerating disproportionately because of immigration, particularly of Nepalese peoples, but also to some extent of Bengalis and others. This has resulted in the replacement of practically all natural habitat up to, and frequently beyond, declared forest boundaries.

The forest belt where the pygmy hog occurs is a semi-continuous series of forest and thatchland areas that run from eastern North Bengal to Upper Assam. It is intersected by tributaries of the Brahmaputra, and is divided into Reserve Forests, Unclassed State Forests, and two wildlife sanctuaries, Manas and Sonai-Rupa.

**The small size and perfect streamlining of the pygmy hog are excellent adaptations for the very dense habitat in which it lives**

An adult male pygmy hog photographed in captivity on a tea estate in northern Assam. Attempts to breed pygmy hogs in captivity have not met with a great deal of success so far, and their best hope for survival still lies with the preservation of protected areas of thatch-scrub in the wild

Neither Reserve Forests nor Unclassed State Forests are regarded as wildlife areas. Essentially, Reserve Forests are geared towards commercial exploitation by the Forest Department. Primary forest is felled for timber extraction and thatchland areas are given over to plantations of commercial species. Most of the thatchland areas are also subject to annual harvesting for thatch ('thatch-mahal') under permits issued by the Forest Department. Thatch is a very important building material which is used for roofing for the vast majority of dwellings in Assam. Some Reserve Forests also have grazing concessions, and some have sand and stone extraction concessions.

The Unclassed State Forests which are interspersed between the Reserve Forests do not have an afforestation program and are not actively managed by the Forest Department; most of them are being progressively encroached upon and are unlikely to survive as forest areas. On the whole, settlement in Reserve Forests and Unclassed State Forests is actually encroachment, but there are official settlements, particularly in the Unclassed State Forests. In some places little or no action has been taken against illegal settlement.

These processes have a particularly serious effect on the thatchland and scrub jungles, which are highly susceptible to human disturbance, particularly by dry-season burning. This habitat (unlike the true forests) has now become discontinuous and forms a series of vulnerable units within the declared forest boundaries. Moreover, these thatchland areas tend to be along the southern edge of the forests and are therefore often in particularly close proximity to human habitation.

Burning of the thatchlands is probably the single most important factor affecting the pygmy hog. It is not a new phenomenon—it has been practised for generations, and the species has survived. But the situation is different today, as few areas are now remote enough to be safe from regular burning. Moreover, although burning is a tradition of long standing, its disastrous effects on wildlife have not been appreciated, and these effects are also exacerbated by other factors. Burning is either 'controlled' burning in plots by forest officials or later 'accidental' or uncontrolled burning by local people. This accidental burning is either caused by carelessness—herdsmen cooking or smoking in the forest—or by deliberate firing to improve grazing and thatch yield. But however caused, burning is incompatible with the survival of resident species like the pygmy hog, and has had ecologically disastrous consequences for them.

As burning completely destroys all cover and most food stuffs it obviously serves to keep the pygmy hog population at a low level—directly proportional to the amount of habitat left unburnt. Small remaining areas of unburnt habitat are isolated in the post-burning period prior to the regrowth of vegetation after the rains, so that other factors, such as hunting, are concentrated on them and further reduce the remaining resident pygmy hog population. But annual burning is still an official Forest Department policy in many areas, partly as an aid to forestry and partly to prevent burning by other people at a later date which would be more harmful to forest plantations. Pygmy hogs and other species that are displaced by the burning of their habitat have to seek refuge elsewhere and there is no suitable alternative habitat available, hence their appearance on tea plantations at this time of year. By the very nature of the unsuitability of this habitat, coupled with hunting pressure, it is very unlikely that any of these animals will survive.

Burning is also undertaken by villagers and herdsmen to improve grazing for domestic herbivores, sometimes legally, sometimes not. And even in the wildlife sanctuaries burning is undertaken by the authorities both because controlled burning is less destructive than uncontrolled accidental burning later in the year, and also to provide more fodder for wild herbivores. The latter argument is extremely dubious as fodder is hardly likely to be in short supply in a high grass habitat (except, perhaps ironically, after burning!) and even if successful it would lead to the artificial maintenance of an over-optimum population of a few species at the expense of many others. The Manas Sanctuary, which is probably the most important area for the future conservation of pygmy hogs, is extensively and deliberately burnt by the forest officials even though it does not support a very heavy population of grazing ungulates.

Hunting or poaching is another cause of mortality, as mentioned earlier. The isolation of small unburnt areas greatly facilitates hunting as men can be deployed only in these areas and can screen randomly for game, set snares

The color of the pygmy hog is blackish-brown, shaded with ginger, and the hairs are quite sparsely distributed compared with those of a wild boar. Hunting for the pot (center) is still a threat to the pygmy hog, particularly because it tends to be concentrated in small remnant populations which are left after dry-season burning has destroyed most of the habitat. Several of the animals rediscovered in 1971 had severe leg injuries (the one in the bottom picture has lost a leg) having been caught in gin traps: three died within a short time or gin traps, or drive animals out of cover. Pygmy hogs are still regularly hunted though they are rarely sold in bazaars now, as they are likely to be recognized by forest officials, and the hunters and retailers are liable to be prosecuted. However, poaching is not severe in all Reserve Forests, and in the Manas Sanctuary it is probably not serious as other game is more profitable—and in any case anti-poaching measures have reduced poaching significantly.

Other sources of disturbance include such illegal activities as collection of forest vegetables and firewood, and domestic thatch collection out of season; some areas also have by-ways through the forest which are used by local people. While not a serious threat in themselves, these practices greatly increase the chances of accidental burning of the small and precious remaining patches of unburnt habitat.

While no attempt has been made to estimate the total population of the pygmy hog, it is unlikely that there are more than 150 to 200 animals left in Assam and there could well be considerably less than this. The fact that the 'thatchlands' are essentially flat, well-drained savanna, which is ideal for forestry and agriculture, has meant a disproportionate loss of habitat for the pygmy hog over its entire former range. As I have said, not only have the processes of settlement and encroachment reduced the former habitat areas up to or even inside forest boundaries, but the vast majority of whatever natural habitat remains in these areas is further despoiled by burning and other forestry practices.

One reason for the acute situation facing the pygmy hog is that the surviving populations are largely confined to Reserve Forests—and these areas are not wildlife areas and within them there is no real policy regarding wildlife conservation. In fact, the Forest Department, which is also responsible for wildlife, is the main agent responsible for the destruction of this habitat, and therefore of the species. The 1972 Indian Wildlife (Protection) Act accorded maximum protection to the pygmy hog, but this protection is mainly concerned with hunting and is anyway poorly enforced and largely unenforceable. Hunting may be a serious threat in some areas but it mainly serves to make worse the situation caused by habitat destruction, and habitat is not legally protected except in declared wildlife areas. Of the latter, only Manas supports pygmy hogs and most of the available habitat there is also destroyed by burning.

Sonai-Rupa, the other wildlife sanctuary in the region, now has no pygmy hogs, though they did occur there about thirty years ago. It has not been maintained or developed as a wildlife area and is also subject to burning by herdsmen who have permanent settlement and grazing rights in the sanctuary. The army leases some sixty-four square kilometers as a firing range and for large-scale troop maneuvers. (It also wants a further area of about the same size.) Sonai-Rupa would still be an ideal place for the reintroduction of pygmy hogs if it could be upgraded to its proper status.

But what is really required is a change of attitude towards dry season burning and its very serious consequences. That the pygmy hog has a precarious future is in no doubt, and positive and rapid action is needed if it is to survive. It would be ironic if the academic reprieve granted to the species by its rediscovery in 1971 should prove to be short lived.

# A HELPING HAND FOR THE ARABIAN GAZELLE

Keith Laidler

'There is but a thin sheet of brown paper between this place and hell.' Such was the comment of an eighteenth-century British sailor on the Sultanate of Oman. And indeed, as I flew into Sib airport on a blisteringly hot January morning I could think of no better description. My brief was to catalogue the more interesting animals of Oman for possible filming, yet at that time I found it very hard to believe that anything but a few insects could survive in that 85,000 square miles of arid, inhospitable terrain.

Oman is virtually an island of mountains, bounded to the east by the Indian Ocean and to the west by an ocean of sand, the infamous Empty Quarter. Rainfall is seasonal and sparse, and the land is cut about with dry river beds or *wadis* that in times of flood can make any sort of travel—even by camel—impossible.

Yet this inhospitable land supports a wealth of small vertebrate life. Amphibians and reptiles are there in abundance, including nine lizard species and six snakes. As late as 1970 three new lizards were discovered in central Oman on the Jebel Akhdar range, which suggests how much zoological work probably remains to be done in this little-studied area. Small mammals are fewer, but even so include such unexpected creatures as the bat-eared Brandt's hedgehog and the white-tailed mongoose.

But strangest of all is the survival of the large mammals. The beautiful Arabian gazelle and the tahr can be found in the more remote areas of the region, and the Arabian leopard (or *Nimer*) somehow manages to pursue its livelihood in the northern mountains, as do the wolf and the wild cat.

However, as the human population increases, so the land available to wildlife decreases in proportion. And as the larger animals need more space than the smaller in which to feed and reproduce, it is the leopard, antelope, and wolf which bear the brunt of man's expansion. Hunting is perhaps the greatest danger of all, and unless there are tighter restrictions on such activity all these beasts seem doomed to extinction in the wild. One species, the Arabian oryx, has already gone—a victim of the 'motorized chase'. This so-called sport is a travesty of true hunting. It involves neither the slow, painstaking tracking of an animal, nor any type of marksmanship. The quarry is simply followed in jeeps or trucks and, when caught, mown down with sub-machine guns.

Having disposed of the oryx, the hunters (who often are not even Omanis, but cross the border from a number of neighboring states) are now turning their attentions to the Arabian gazelle, an animal already listed as endangered in the *Red Data Book* of the International Union for Conservation of Nature. Luckily, however, a start has been made in Oman to protect this attractive antelope.

With the approval of the sultan, His Majesty Quaboos Bin Said, a small reserve has been set up by David Ennals, a British army officer seconded to the sultan's army. The reserve is located about ten bumpy, difficult miles from Muscat in the foothills of the Jebel Aswad. The area is certainly remote: part of the journey (by Land-Rover, the only advisable vehicle in which to travel) is along a rock-strewn watercourse. Even the Land-Rover's four-wheel drive has difficulty here. But the journey is worth it.

Some time before I had spent a fruitless two days searching for the Arabian gazelle on Goat Island, off the Musandam Peninsula. Although we found what were probably tracks and droppings of gazelles, we saw no sign of the elusive animals—despite the fact that the island itself is no more than half a mile long.

But now we rounded a bend after our bumpy drive, and there, beneath a small village, were two pens containing five or six superb gazelles.

The Arabian gazelle must rate as one of the most attractive of all antelopes. Its long delicate face is very appealing and the twin bands of white and black which run along either side of the face from eye to muzzle give the creature a very superior, almost aristocratic appearance

**Very little is known of the biology and behavior of the Arabian gazelle. It does not seem to travel in large groups, but this may be because it is now so rare**

when seen at close range. All the gazelle species are very similar and one distinguishing characteristic is the shape and size of the horns. In the male Arabian gazelle the horns are rather short, about six to ten inches long from base to tip, and usually hook both forwards and inwards, although this feature is very variable. The female's horns are even less impressive (from three-and-a-half to six inches long) and are very slender and not so divergent as those of the male. Their moderate size—they rarely exceed a height of two feet at the shoulder—and long legs with small black hooves render them perfectly adapted to the rocky hill country in which they live. Their coloration, too, a light rufous with dark flank and rump stripes, makes them all but invisible against the reddish-brown rocks and shadows of the Omani mountains. Small wonder that we had failed to come upon them in our slow wanderings among the rocks of Goat Island.

The evasiveness of the gazelle and the harsh environment in which it lives have combined to make this species one of the least studied of the antelope family. Very little is known of its biology and behavior. It is not usually a gregarious creature and is normally seen in bands of four or five, at most. This may, however, be a result of it now being so rare, for according to David Harrison, an authority on the mammals of the Arabian Peninsula in areas such as Dhofar where it is still relatively common, quite large herds are occasionally seen.

The gazelles are believed to feed on a wide variety of plant food, and are said to be capable of existing in their arid habitat without drinking. In fact, many other species of gazelles have this capacity. In Africa, Grant's gazelles have been seen to feed from certain dry shrubs during times of drought. Analysis has shown that the shrubs absorb water from the air during the hours of darkness when the relative humidity of the atmosphere is greater. By feeding at night the gazelles are able to get all the water they need. Presumably the Arabian gazelle will also have such specialized abilities in its behavioral repertoire.

Almost nothing is known about reproduction in this species. On the fertile Batinah Coast of Oman the gazelle appears to breed twice a year, giving birth in January and late July. In Palestine, however, it is reported that the animal's main birth period is the spring. In fact, in periods of very severe drought they do

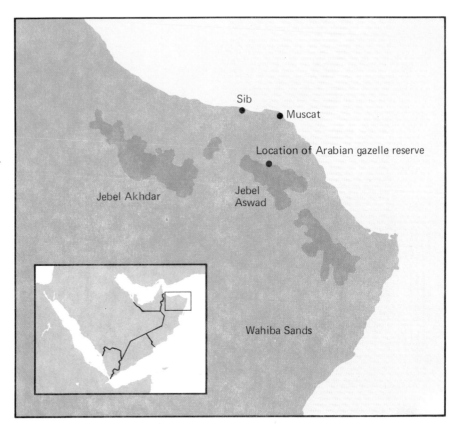

not seem to breed at all. These differences are probably adaptations to the vagaries of the climate in that part of the world. From a species survival point of view, it is pointless for the female to waste valuable resources in producing a fawn which in difficult conditions has little chance of survival.

Although very widely distributed throughout the Arabian Peninsula, the species *Gazella gazella* is spread quite thinly on the ground. The Jebel Aswad reserve is therefore of great importance in the survival of the species as a whole, and especially of the two sub-species found in Oman, *G.g. arabica* and *G.g. muscatensis*.

It is to be hoped that this small experimental station can continue to expand. At present there is one full-time warden who is responsible for feeding and watering the dozen or so gazelles, but more resources and men must surely be necessary if the station is to fulfil its potential and become a successful breeding center for this endangered species. It would be a very great pity to see the reserve, and with it perhaps the Arabian gazelle itself, vanish into the rocks and sand of Oman.

One of the most attractive of all antelopes, the Arabian gazelle has been severely hunted despite its relatively unimpressive horns. However, they are not easy to see as their light rufous coloring makes them almost invisible in the rocky mountains of the Arabian Peninsula. Hope for the future survival of the species is represented by the Jebel Aswad reserve, where these pictures were taken, some ten miles from Muscat in the Sultanate of Oman

# WHAT FUTURE FOR THE ELEPHANT?

Iain Douglas-Hamilton

The African elephant is seriously threatened in some areas—a fact that is obvious to almost every layman. But a precise, scientifically-based calculation of the overall status of elephants has not yet been undertaken. Among the important questions which require investigation and fully detailed answers are:

Which areas, in which countries, are losing elephants, and why?
How does mortality divide between poaching and other causes such as drought, range depletion, over-concentration in national parks, and natural die-off?
What are the trends in elephant birth-rate?
What are the precise mechanics of the ivory trade, country by country?
How do the authorities in the various countries calculate the economic value of an elephant—in terms of profit to private enterprise from meat and ivory, or as a self-sustaining resource producing a continuous income for the national exchequer through tourism?
Is there any official appreciation, anywhere in Africa, of the elephant's value in terms of concepts such as aesthetics, culture, science, national pride, and the national heritage?

An ambitious attempt to answer these questions has now been started, with the launching of a joint three-year project by the International Union for Conservation of Nature (IUCN) and the World Wildlife Fund (WWF). Overall director of the project is Dr Iain Douglas-Hamilton. He and Dr Harvey Croze are concentrating on the African elephant, while Dr J. C. Daniel and Mr R. Olivier are studying the elephant in Asia.

In this article we look at the initial results of the work of Iain Douglas-Hamilton and his colleagues in Africa. The program began with the distribution of a questionnaire to official and private sources. It was hoped that by this means, supplemented by direct field research, it would be possible to establish current elephant ranges, produce initial population estimates, and determine the main trends in elephant population dynamics. The paradox of elephant decimation in most areas and over-concentration in certain parks and reserves is receiving immediate and special attention. The project team expects to be able to suggest monitoring and control measures in respect of destruction and modification of elephant habitats, which could involve recommendations for culling or cropping.

Much of the research work will be done by experts in the field and other specialists, with study areas selected according to the following criteria:

1 Areas where elephants are thought to be endangered.
2 Areas representative of important habitats.
3 Little-known areas with no research facilities but where large elephant populations are thought to exist.
4 Areas with a special history of man-elephant-habitat interaction.
5 Areas with current active research programs.
6 Areas where previous intensive research needs updating.

Each elephant population of any size will be viewed in relation to existing plans for the development of agriculture or tourism so as to provide a realistic scale of priorities for conservation recommendations.

The last phase of the project will be to devise a conservation action program with specific recommendations on management, training, and public information schemes; continuing research and monitoring; the strengthening of wildlife administrations; the creation of new parks and reserves, and so on. Another aim is to examine the feasibility of establishing a cartel of ivory-producing nations in order to regulate the trade, stabilize prices, and foster a more rational approach to sustaining the resource through conservation.

The 'elephant situation' is looked on by

**The African elephant is probably that continent's best known animal. But like so many other large mammals (it is in fact the world's largest land animal) its numbers are declining and it is seriously threatened with extinction in some areas**

some as a test case in the sense that if this skirmish to preserve one species can be won, then it will give grounds for optimism that the overall battle for conservation of Africa's natural resources and environment is worthwhile. In one area already surveyed there is very definitely cause for optimism. This is the giant Selous Game Reserve in Tanzania—at 55,000 square kilometers (21,000 square miles) the largest in Africa—which now supports at least 80,000 of a possible total elephant population in Tanzania of half a million.

The first phase of the project has now been completed, with support from the New York Zoological Society. Although the continental picture is still very far from complete, and in most cases it is not yet possible to hazard a guess at elephant numbers within a given country, our knowledge of the African elephant has advanced and current information (even if a bit sketchy) on elephant distribution can be shown on a map. This map is a first draft, and will certainly be amended and added to as the project progresses. The complexity of the overall status of elephants in Africa can be judged from the following summary of the preliminary research.

**Angola** Dr Brian Huntly has provided pre-September 1975 information, from which is plotted the elephants' recent distribution, and since then reports have come in from other sources. During the conflict armed men of the three political factions entered national parks and reserves and destroyed elephants and other animals, such as giant sable, with automatic weapons. The current situation is unknown.

**Botswana** Dr Von Richter, recent Director of Wildlife, National Parks and Tourism, reports that 'illegal trade in ivory does not present a problem, primarily due to the low human population density, and the fact that the elephant populations are mostly found away from any large human population concentration . . . Elephants are hunted on license by recreational and tribal hunters under a quota system . . . The general attitude of the Government is based on rational utilization of the resource, and the rural population more or less goes along with it; clashes between elephants and people occur only where arable agriculture is carried out.'

Most of the elephants are found in the north of the country, where they are studied both in the Okavango swamps and in the north-east by

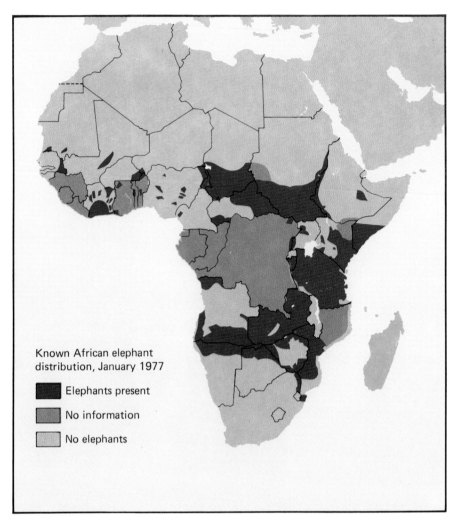

Known African elephant distribution, January 1977

▉ Elephants present

▓ No information

░ No elephants

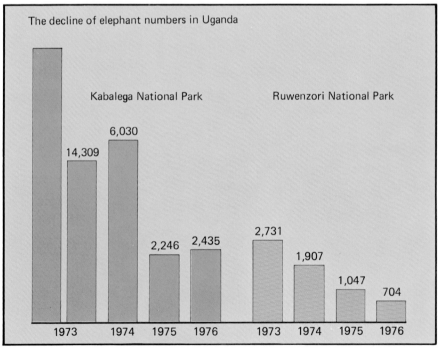

The decline of elephant numbers in Uganda

Kabalega National Park       Ruwenzori National Park

14,309   6,030   2,246   2,435       2,731   1,907   1,047   704

1973   1974   1975   1976       1973   1974   1975   1976

These animals were photographed in Kenya with poachers' arrows embedded in their skin. Poaching is the main cause of declining numbers, and it is especially serious in Kenya. The elephants are killed mainly for their valuable tusks, but the meat is also important

FAO research teams. 'A relict group of elephants of no less than 800 is also found in the Tuli Block and will be studied by staff of the "Endangered Wildlife Trust".' The Tuli Block is of special interest because it appears from the records that elephants were eradicated from this area by early ivory hunters, but they have now successfully recolonized the area, with the first animals reappearing in the 1940s. Secondly, the Tuli Block is one of the few privately owned places in Africa which has a thriving elephant population. Finally, the creation of artificial water points may have affected the distribution of elephants, and the intensity of damage to trees.

**Chad** In the last twenty years the human population of Chad has doubled and the elephant population, together with other wildlife, has been diminishing. It is also one of the poorest of African countries and suffers from the presence of armed rebels who roam over large areas. Chad authorities freely admit that local resources cannot meet the challenge of effective wildlife protection, and so they must rely on outside assistance. Nevertheless, Chad has established a new reserve to protect the addax and the scimitar-horned oryx, and has made great efforts to maintain it. This gesture is especially important as in the past the last greater kudu were destroyed by rockets fired from helicopters—and the same system was used to shoot down elephants.

**Ivory Coast** Elephants are still widely distributed but numbers are decreasing very rapidly. The law decrees total protection but poaching is rife, especially by foreigners from neighboring countries. An informant reports that 'if draconian measures are not taken in the immediate future for protecting this animal, the Ivory Coast will need to change its name.'

**Kenya** A report is being compiled from the multiple sources available, which because of the considerable current research efforts will probably be more detailed than for most other countries in Africa.

It has recently come to light that the famous elephant Ahmed, who died in 1974, had traces of an old bullet wound. It appears that the bullet entered from the left back of the skull and lodged in the root of the right tusk. It is possible that the bullet may have damaged the roots of the left teeth, since the teeth were far less worn down on the left, which may have been because it was painful for Ahmed to chew on that side. The wound was judged to be about five to ten years old, which would mean that he was shot a few years before he was given presidential protection in 1970. That he was shot within the protected area of Marsabit shows how necessary more stringent methods of law enforcement have become.

**Mauritania**  The situation in Mauritania today is absolutely unknown. Naturalists have not visited the area where elephants were known to exist for fifteen years. It is not even known if they still exist there. Droppings were seen, however, in 1971! These elephants, if they survive, are the northernmost on the African continent.

**Rwanda**  This country has the densest human population in Africa and still has a population of 100 to 150 elephants living in the Nyungwe forest on the Zaire border. Until the beginning of 1975 another 150 elephants also lived in the Bugesora area. 'The competition between these animals and man had come to such a pitch and was worsening rapidly (ten per cent of elephants wounded by snares, thirty per cent severely mutilated, crops damaged, small-holders terrorized, etc.) that the Government declared a 'final solution' to the problem. All the elephants were slaughtered except for twenty-six young animals aged from one to eleven years old who were captured and transported to the Akagera Park.'

**Tanzania**  Intensive poaching of elephants, especially in the north, is of great concern, but as the Selous survey showed, elephants are abundant in the south. The dry season count totalled more than 110,000 elephants. Tanzania is one of the greatest reservoirs of elephants in Africa, and the Government has a strong policy on conservation. Analysis of records in the 'Ivory Room' in Dar es Salaam showed that three to four thousand elephants are killed each year in defense of human life and property.

The average weight of a sample of 3,080 tusks was 4.81 kilograms. This was lower than expected, and if it is similar in other countries it may be necessary to revise upwards the estimates of numbers of elephants represented by ivory imported into Hong Kong and elsewhere.

**Uganda**  Dr Keith Eltringham and his colleague Mr R. C. Malpas of the Uganda Institute of Ecology made the fourth annual count of elephants in the Ruwenzori and Kabalega National Parks in September 1976. The results showed a further drastic decline in Ruwenzori, though the Kabalega picture is more encouraging. The number of elephants in Ruwenzori (formerly Queen Elizabeth National Park) has declined from 2,731 in 1973 to 704 in 1976. Numbers are therefore only a quarter of what they were three years earlier, and the high proportion of dead elephants found during the survey suggests that poaching continues unabated—a conclusion supported by the wardens. If this trend continues there will be no elephants left in Ruwenzori within a few years.

The total for Kabalega (formerly Murchison National Park) was 2,435, or about the same as the 2,246 recorded in 1975. The difference of 189 is well within the 'confidence limits' of the totals, so that no significant change has occurred. But the present total should be set against the figure for 1973 of 14,309, which may mean that poaching has eased in the Kabalega region. However, the counting technique is not altogether reliable at such low densities.

**Zambia**  Dr Graeme Caughley, a biologist working for FAO, estimated 350,000 elephants for the whole of Zambia in 1972, with about 100,000 of these in the Luangwa Valley where he thought that they might be increasing. However, poaching has increased since then, though not yet on an East African scale. More recently an official of the Zambian National Parks and Wildlife Service has said: 'The Zambian elephant's existence is seriously threatened by increased poaching, reduction of its natural range, and habitat damage.'

These examples represent some of the information now filed by country and area. Out of a total of twenty-one countries, only five appear to have stable elephant populations and the others are all declining. The most complete information comes from South Africa, and this

Of a total of twenty-one
African countries surveyed,
only five seem to have stable
elephant populations. In all the
others numbers are going down

(Over page) The massive and
frequently destructive strength
of the elephant is rightly
feared by the Africans, but it
is man, with his love of ivory,
who is the greater destroyer

may indicate a pattern for the future.

**South Africa** Most South African elephants were destroyed before the twentieth century. When the Dutch first arrived in 1652 elephants were plentiful around Table Mountain. Within a hundred years they had been wiped out within a 200-mile radius. After the passage of another century elephants had been exterminated in the Cape Province, Orange Free State, Natal, and the Transvaal, except for a few small pockets in the Kruger National Park, Addo, and Knysna in the Tsitsikama Forest. The destruction of South Africa's elephants and other wildlife in the nineteenth century was on a scale unsurpassed on the continent and rivalled the eradication of the bison in North America.

There is only one large elephant population in South Africa today. This is in the Kruger National Park, where they have built up from less than 100 to about 7,275 animals; they are stabilized at that level by culling. According to Dr Salmon Joubert, Chief Research Biologist, culling quotas each year vary with population trends and local environmental conditions. Initial culling was aimed at achieving a population of between 7,000 and 7,500. Future annual cropping will be around 200 to 400 animals: should the elephant population drop below 7,000 the cropping program will be discontinued. 'It must be emphasized', he says, 'that cropping of elephants is solely related to management of the population. Commercial cropping is not a goal in itself. Ivory obtained from cropping operations is traded, and illegal trade in ivory is not known to occur. Illegal hunting is virtually non-existent.'

The Addo Elephant National Park is a small area of 7,735 hectares (19,113 acres) situated in south-eastern Cape Province. The park lies in a region of dense, succulent evergreen thicket, and together with the Knysna Forests, gives sanctuary to the southernmost elephants in Africa. Persecution of the Addo elephants started with the arrival of ivory hunters and white settlers in the late eighteenth century. By the time the park was established in 1931 it had a population of only eleven elephants. But these animals continued to wander in and out of the park, to the annoyance of the surrounding farmers. Then in 1952–4 the warden, Graham Armstrong, erected his now famous fence of railroad lines and the remaining eighteen elephants were enclosed in an area of 2,270

27

hectares (5,609 acres). Thanks to a variety of factors, including early maturity of the females and abundant food, the population has grown fourfold to over eighty elephants. Unfortunately, this population increase has been accompanied by the inevitable habitat destruction so typical of nearly every African park in which the species lives. But a scientific research program is underway, which should result in the establishment of realistic population limits—thus ensuring the continued well-being of a now secure, viable population of elephants.

The north-eastern border area of South Africa, bounded by Swaziland, Mozambique, and the Indian Ocean is known locally as Tongaland. The central part of Tongaland is a refuge for some of the last elephants living outside a protected area in South Africa. There are about twenty to thirty of them, probably all bulls, and though some are resident, others wander to and fro across the border into Mozambique. That they have survived at all is due to the remoteness of the areas which they frequent, and the absence of roads and settlements until very recently. Due to settlement, development, and political tensions in the region, the future prospects for these animals are not encouraging. The only hope would seem to be the construction of an Addo-type fence (an exorbitantly expensive undertaking) and the introduction of females from other areas.

The Knysna elephants live in a large and dense forest. Despite a main road running through the forest and the proximity of numerous settlements, the elephants are so secretive that they are very seldom seen. Only ten to fourteen animals survive, and their numbers seem to have remained stable since 1925 when they were last thoroughly counted. Some authorities feel that poaching is to be blamed for the fact that numbers are not increasing, as at Addo. However, the Forestry Department disagrees and feels that herding the elephants into a limited fenced area would be too risky for them, and puts forward the view that they are probably in balance with their environment.

Dr Joubert sums up thus: 'I certainly do not regard the elephant as endangered or threatened in southern Africa (South Africa, Rhodesia, Botswana, Mozambique, and Zambia). Their future must be regarded as secure, provided

the various populations are managed scientifically and political stability in the countries concerned can provide effective law enforcement.'

From slaughter to strict preservation and management of a remnant: could the South African example be the pattern for the future elsewhere on this continent? Or can the rest of Africa at the eleventh hour halt the killing, and preserve elephants within wider and more balanced ecosystems? And would a more *laissez faire* policy still be appropriate in some of these areas, while in others a sustained yield cropping were carried out?

In the field, it is possible to get an idea of recent trends by recording all dead elephants, and calculating a ratio of dead to live. This technique is in effect an 'on-going body count' to monitor continuing human predation and other causes of death. Body counts can also suggest variation in the death rate between different areas. For instance, in the dry season it was found that within the Selous Game Reserve the ratio of dead to live elephants was 4:100, whereas outside the reserve it was 9:100. In Meru National Park in Kenya the ratio was 6:100, while outside the park boundaries it was

**Bull elephants drinking. The dead trees have been killed by elephants stripping off the bark**

**The destruction of trees has become much more noticeable since elephants have been protected in national parks where they are relatively safe from human persecution**

as high as 70:100. It appears that human predation was responsible, in both cases, for the higher ratio of dead to live animals outside the protected areas.

The main problem in interpreting this data is that carcasses disappear at different rates depending on rainfall, insects which eat the body, and the density of predators. In the Serengeti predators tend to devour the flesh and scatter the bones so that very little remains two months after death – whereas in the drier parts of Tsavo a full skeleton may endure for ten years or more. Nevertheless, by looking for a rotting patch where putrefying flesh has killed the grass, it is often possible to identify a recent corpse even when the skin is absent and the bones are scattered.

Useful data can also come from small populations of 'known' elephants, such as those at Manyara in Tanzania, Amboseli in Kenya, and Addo in South Africa. In these cases it is possible to record all births and deaths, family by family, thus enabling precise trends to be calculated. Long-term studies are now in progress in these three areas which will monitor the response of these elephants to changing conditions.

The development of computer simulation models to further analyse the information and to predict future trends will be helpful, as will a program being developed to simulate the exploitation of ivory and its effect on elephants in pre-colonial Africa.

Broadly speaking, the objectives of the first phase of the elephant project have been achieved – with just two disappointments. Not all the African nations responded to the request for information on elephant dynamics, and (predictably) hard facts on ivory trading were scarce. But these two problems were being tackled in the second phase, which was underway as this was written.

# THE ADAPTABLE LEOPARD

Norman Myers

Prior to human modification of its habitats on a large scale, the leopard enjoyed a wide distribution in Africa, and good numbers. The disruptive process became apparent in North Africa and South Africa by the start of the twentieth century, though it is a measure of the leopard's adaptability that it survived in both areas long after the lion had been generally eliminated. The next two regions to be affected were West Africa and Somalia, although the leopard withstood the process better than most mammal species, despite the loss of its preferred prey and the general deterioration of the environment, which led to a decrease in its range and numbers.

Elsewhere the leopard's status remained satisfactory until at least the end of World War II. After that the broad-scale use of modern medicine for humans and livestock triggered an accelerated change in wildland environments. And so, despite its capacity for adaptation, the leopard began to decline over wide tracts of Africa. An indication of the trend is the example of Kenya, where the leopard's main prey species, such as small antelopes, started to disappear from ranchlands – followed shortly thereafter by the leopard itself.

One result of the intensification of agriculture is that farmers, especially in South Africa, have been inclined to see the leopard not as a species deserving some protection except under certain circumstances, but rather as a creature to be treated as vermin and eliminated almost out of duty. Regrettably this attitude seems to be spreading in southern Africa, although a sounder objective would be to maintain the highest number and widest possible distribution of leopards without leading to unacceptable conflict with livestock interests. In other words,

although the livestock industry has legitimate interests which deserve protection, wholesale predator control (in effect elimination) is not necessarily the best way to achieve this aim.

Predator control needs to be viewed as no more than one aspect of predator management, which in itself should be planned as part of an overall policy of natural resource conservation for the welfare of society as a whole. Within this context, it is plain that unselective methods such as the use of poison should have no place except in extreme circumstances.

The application of more intensive rangeland practices is already spreading to Masailand in East Africa, to Somalia, to Ethiopia, and parts of West Africa, and some predator species will certainly undergo some reduction in some areas for some periods; but a more discretionary and selective strategy needs to replace the indiscriminate approach which characterizes southern Africa's response to predators, if the widest possible spectrum of resources is to be maintained.

Another factor, which may actually affect the cheetah more than the leopard, is the spread of what may be termed semi-subsistence agriculture. The upsurge in human numbers, linked to a still more powerful phenomenon – the upsurge in human aspirations – is evident in part through a population overspill from more fertile areas into savanna zones. This is already apparent in several countries, and is likely to become so in many others.

Technology may help to check the process by permitting more concentrated cultivation of cash crops in highly fertile areas, but on the other hand technology aids the taking up of land in savannas through developments such as drought-resistant strains of maize. Ultimately the habitat modifications involved must constrict the life-support systems of the leopard, though less so and less quickly than it does for other predators and many herbivorous animals.

The activities of the international fur trade have severely aggravated the pressures I have already described. The furriers may not have considered it to be their business to support protection programs and assist in solutions for the highly complex problem of assuring the conservation of a common property resource, the leopard.

This attitude is different, however, from actively conniving in the evasion of controls,

**The agile leopard has no difficulty climbing trees, though its hunting is done on the ground. The leopard has been affected by the disappearance of its preferred prey species, such as small antelopes, over large areas of Africa**

as has all too often been the case. For at least fifteen years the industry must have been aware that in certain areas the resource was under unsustainable pressure by virtue of fur market demands. Yet, to cite only the case of the so-called Somali leopard, the industry has not investigated whether market indications called for curbs on the excessive exploitation of this particular form of leopard. Instead, the reaction of furriers was to lay their hands on any skin available, regardless of price and regardless of the cost to Somali leopard populations. In short, the trade's operations have been inefficient to an extreme degree, both ecologically and economically.

The numbers of leopards for which the fur trade may have accounted in the recent past is hard to estimate, given the reluctance of competitive interests within the industry to divulge even rough figures of turnover. However, US Department of Commerce statistics show that 9,556 leopard skins were imported into the United States in 1968, and 7,934 in 1969. Among these were a few from Asia, but mainly they came from Ethiopia, Kenya, and South Africa. Furthermore, it is generally agreed in the trade that for every skin leaving Africa another is rejected as useless because of damage or poor curing; some leopards are destroyed by hyenas before the trapper gets to them; and, if a female with a litter is killed, the death of the cubs must also be accounted as a loss directly attributable to the trade. Altogether, the total offtake in 1968 and 1969 could have been of the order of 50,000 each year.

In 1970 imports by the United States and in 1972 by Britain tailed off markedly as a consequence of new controls, but in 1973 the demand for skins from continental Europe was said to surpass that of the late 1960s – thereby bringing the level back again to some 50,000 a year.

It is the concentration of this demand upon certain localities which has led to gross over-exploitation in several countries, when a more even spread over the leopard's whole range might have had less serious consequences. On the other hand, the impact has sometimes been localized to the extent that it causes depletion of leopard numbers in only a single sector of a country, such as Ngamiland in Botswana and Barotseland in Zambia.

What, then, is being done to conserve the leopard? Conservation measures have mainly

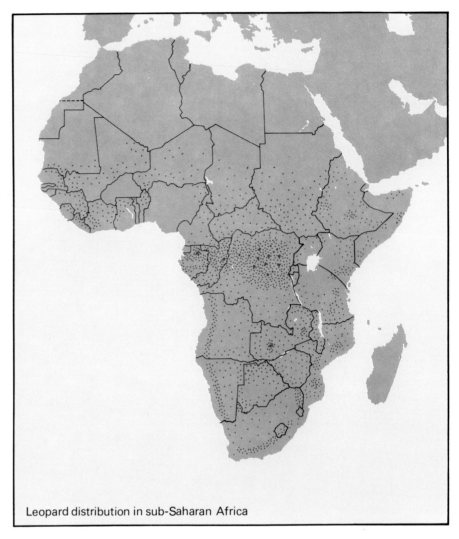

Leopard distribution in sub-Saharan Africa

The leopard's beautifully patterned coat was a major reason for its decline. Public opinion in many countries is now changing, and in addition new laws now prohibit the trade in leopard skins, so the prospects for its survival are brighter than they once seemed

depended up to now on legislative protection of the species itself and reservation of its habitat. Looking at the first point, most countries of sub-Saharan Africa now extend some degree of legal protection to the leopard. Although only ratified by about half the signatories, the African Convention of 1968, while permitting some forms of exploitation such as sport hunting, prohibits commercial dealings in skins. This, at any rate, was the position reached in most countries by 1974, though several had by then outlawed all forms of exploitation including licensed hunting.

(Published figures indicate that the total continent-wide offtake by sport hunters has probably not exceeded 500 a year during the past few years. In areas of satisfactory leopard density, sport hunting could be encouraged as a highly lucrative form of land use – though it tends to raise difficulties if, at the same time, local people are forbidden to molest the leopard even for the protection of their livestock.)

Regulations vary from country to country in detail and in the frequency with which they are changed. This confusing situation should be partially resolved now that the Washington Convention (the Convention on International Trade in Endangered Species of Wild Fauna and Flora) has come into force in a number of African countries. This is because the convention's schedules require that exploitation of the leopard and trade in its skin be totally prohibited – which may seem hard on a stock-raising community which suffers appreciable livestock losses from leopards. It may even seem hard, in some people's view, on certain segments of the fur trade. But in the light of the pressures that the stockmen and the fur trade currently direct at the leopard, the leopard's position in the top protected category of the convention seems justified, and should not be altered unless provisions can be made to eliminate substantial attrition in numbers resulting from these two sources.

There remains the problem of law enforcement. Few countries have the resources to finance and staff wildlife protection in the way they would wish. Tanzania, for instance, has recently been spending a higher proportion of its budget on wildlife conservation than the United States (though like the United States, it achieves only moderate success in controlling poaching). But all too often light sentences are

**The leopard often stores its prey in trees, where it is safe from the attentions of other animals**

imposed on those who offend against the wildlife laws. However, confiscation of skins, traps, guns, and vehicles serves as a sound deterrent. This measure is at present applied only rarely, though it would not be unfair if it were always applied.

The countries of sub-Saharan Africa have established over 150 parks and reserves, with a total area nearly twice that of Great Britain. In many cases they offer favorable or even optimal habitats for leopards; very few are likely to contain no leopards, and at a rough guess they extend protection to at least 50,000, possibly many more. At the same time, many protected areas are by no means assured of a stable future, particularly in savanna zones.

This is due not only to the problems posed by human population growth in surrounding areas, but also to adverse environmental factors. For example, much of the woodland in the Kabalega National Park in Uganda has been converted to grassland by elephants and fire, which must have affected the park's carrying capacity for leopard. And in Amboseli Park in Kenya a rise in the water table and subsequent increase in soil salinity has killed off acacia woodlands, with similar consequences for the leopards.

**The coat which so attracts the fur trade does have an important value for the leopard itself—it gives excellent camouflage, and is one of the factors which enable the leopard to survive in a wide range of habitats**

# FRIENDLY KILLER

Erich Hoyt

'Kawoof!' – The sound was behind me, the sound of a whale breathing. 'Kawoof! Kawoof!' Two more – I was surrounded. It was a misty early morning off Canada's west coast, off northern Vancouver Island. Just me and my rowboat and three killer whales.

I sat motionless, watching them rise quickly from the water, blow, then disappear again. My heart started pounding. The largest whale was three times the size of my dinghy and he was zeroing in. I knew in seconds we would be eyeball to eyeball, or something. . .

I peered down over the side of the boat, through the dark green water. Suddenly the whale appeared, twenty feet below, pushing quickly towards the surface. A strange satisfying calm enveloped me. Then the water broke and the surfacing leviathan erupted in a wave that lifted me and my boat high above the water. He was about six feet away and I could almost touch him. Then he blew with a great 'kawoof'. The spray covered me, soothing like a cool shower on a hot day, and I *was* sweating!

I tried to stabilize the boat. The whale sucked air into his massive body – a hollow, cavernous sucking sound – and rolled on his side. And for an instant he seemed to be staring at me – with that dark penetrating eye of a killer whale.

That was my initiation – that day in early July 1973 – into the world of a fabled and feared creature called 'killer', a creature which, despite his fierce name and reputation, I will always consider a friend.

For the last five summers, I have taken part in expeditions to film, record and study *Orcinus orca*, the largest member of the dolphin family, in its natural habitat. During that time we have approached closer than we ever thought possible, concentrating on one pod, or

family group, of twenty whales called Stubbs's pod (named after an older whale with a distinctive stubby dorsal fin). The stories we had heard about this up to thirty-foot-long, nine-ton marine mammal, far-fetched as they often were, possessed at least a grain of truth. But do the animals merit being called 'killers'?

Yes and no. Carnivorous like man, with no natural predators, killer whales have their choice of fare in the sea. They roam every ocean in the world, their diet varying according to locality. Fish and squid are the mainstay, followed by dolphins, other whales, seals, sealions, and seabirds. The name 'killer whale' is derived from 'whale-killer', coined by nineteenth-century whalers when they observed it killing and eating baleen whales. In some parts of the South Atlantic and Indian Oceans, *orcas* reportedly feed almost exclusively on lesser rorquals, specifically minke whales. There are many documented accounts from around the world of killer whales showing a preference for the lips and tongues of large whales. Some of these reports have come from the British Columbia coast, near our study area.

In May 1964, biologist David Hancock and two companions spent over three hours watching the slaughter of a minke whale stranded at low tide in Barkley Sound, Vancouver Island. Three adult male killer whales waged the forty-five-minute attack, while two females each with a calf waited in the wings. After it was over, the entire pod fed on the sunken carcass of the twenty-seven-foot minke whale. No blood was detected in the water, but the area was covered with a film of oil. The three men later recovered fragments of tongue and other flesh floating in the water.

The following day, Hancock towed what was left of the carcass to shore and examined it. The tongue had been eaten but the blubber and flesh were left untouched. Most amazing of all, Hancock observed, 'the skin had been neatly ripped off . . . the appearance being that of a freshly peeled orange.' Two months later, in the same region, another minke whale was discovered which had apparently met a similar end.

Surprisingly enough, in Johnstone Strait – our study area, off northeastern Vancouver Island – we have observed the local population of two minke whales and a couple of dozen Dall's porpoises (which are also habitually

A killer whale begins his leap. Despite being a carnivore with no natural enemies (besides man), and the largest member of the dolphin family, the killer whale is no danger to man

eaten by *orcas*) actually swimming in the same area for the last four years, apparently untouched and unperturbed by killer whales. It seems that killer whales here subsist on salmon and other fish and are rarely interested in other marine mammals.

Killer whales have attacked boats on rare occasions but we have never witnessed any hostility, nor experienced the fear that brought Owen Lee (author of a monumental treatise on diving) to write that 'there is no remedy against an attack by a killer whale, except Reincarnation', and encouraged the US Navy Diving Manual to issue *orca* a four star (highest) danger rating. Most of our film footage was shot close-up from a canoe and, if anything, we have noticed careful concern from the whales, when they surface near our small boats, not to upset the flimsy craft. Our experience runs contrary to the widespread image of this so-called killer. And no documented case exists – anywhere – of a killer whale adding man to his diet.

Killer whales have large complex brains, as do all toothed whales, including dolphins, which are comparable in size of cerebral cortex and ratio of brain weight to body weight, to man's brain. Whale 'intelligence' must, of course be very different from man's; our intelligence is often expressed through our hands, while whales have never experienced prehensile development.

'Without benefit of hands or outside constructions of any sort,' suggests California dolphin scientist Dr John C. Lilly, 'they may have taken the path of legends and verbal traditions rather than that of written records.' Whales may be great orators storing detailed histories of the ocean and its inhabitants in their massive brains, able to produce their lineage orally like certain tribes in Africa.

The coastal Indians of British Columbia attribute to the 'blackfish', as they call them, an almost divine intelligence. In Alert Bay, a Kwakiutl stronghold off northern Vancouver Island, I spoke with James Sewid, fisherman and chief. He remarked: 'It is only recently that the white man through his aquariums has recognized the blackfish intelligence. We have known about it for a very long time.'

The seine fishermen, primarily Indian, who hunt for salmon side by side with the killers, appreciate their hunting abilities. They have observed the whales in formation herding the

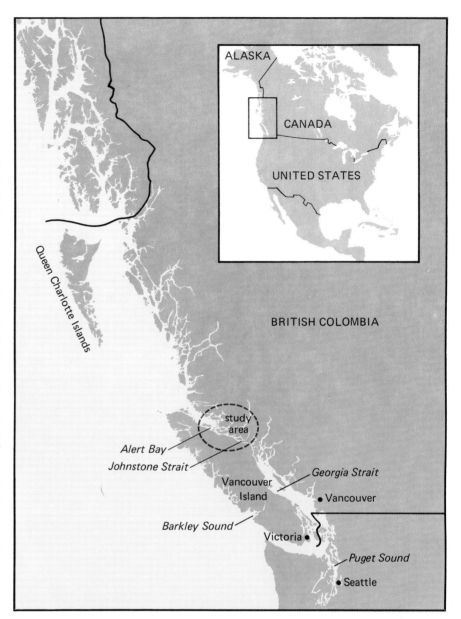

A bull killer whale with calf (above). The calves proved more curious and less fearful than the adult whales. A researcher (left) paddles up to a young killer whale, which seems more interested in playing than in killing. Although it would have been easy for the whales to cause chaos with their antics, they took great care not to rock the boat

salmon in preparation for the kill. Certain seine fishermen describe making their best sets directly in the path of oncoming *orcas*, rounding up the salmon that the whales have herded. Other fishermen are not so lucky. They believe that the whales take advantage of a good set by diving deep and scooping the fish out of their net immediately before it closes. But all who have seen killer whales in action believe they are shrewd, highly skilled hunters.

In June 1973, four of us set sail on the yawl *Four Winds* from Victoria to find, film, and record killer whales along the British Columbia coast. As soundman and a student of electronic music, I was first fascinated by their sonic abilities. Killer whales possess a highly-developed sonar-type navigation system which enables them to find their way and find their food in the murky waters they inhabit. They emit a series of clicking sounds for echo-location purposes and a complex and extremely varied program of whistles, screams, and groans (which are actually speeded-up clicks) for possible communication. Most of their sounds are within man's hearing range, and I recorded their underwater vocalizations with a hydro-phone.

I also brought an electronic music synthe-sizer able to duplicate whale sounds, which I thought might engage the whales' curiosity. I reasoned that since whales use sound so extensively for information gathering and perhaps communication, the ideal way to interest the whales would be through an audio approach. I thought the synthesizer would be more useful than a tape recorder to play back sounds to them; a synthesizer would add a 'human accent' to the whale sound and allow spontaneous live responses.

In the afternoon of 20 July 1973 I played the first imitation whale phrase on the electronic synthesizer's keyboard. The three-note phrase was broadcast through a hull-mounted under-water speaker to Stubbs's pod which had circled our sailboat and now lay on the surface about 200 yards away.

Almost immediately, three or four whales answered – in unison! But what was most astounding was that they had mimicked my imperfect imitation of their sound rather than simply repeating their own phrase. This spontaneous choral mimicry by the wild killer whales occurred three times that first day. But what, were the whales trying to say?

Throughout that first summer and the next summer the synthesizer functioned as a tool which, though often playing to preoccupied *orcas*, occasionally drew whales in close to inspect the hydrophone and the men on the sailboat who were the source of the strange sound. On these special occasions we exchanged vocalizations – sometimes lasting over fifteen-minute periods. But no one yet knows what these sounds mean or if man can really communicate with intelligent life in the sea. Little research has been done beyond Dr Lilly's attempts in the mid-1960s to teach dolphins to speak English. Recently, however, Lilly has decided to return to dolphin research armed with new approaches and predicts that by 1980 we may know whether inter-species communication is possible with whales and dolphins.

In July 1974, writer-photographer James Hunter and I brought a large documentary film production crew to Johnstone Strait. Stubbs's pod had grown by several members, new calves, clearly identifiable from their yellowish ivory coloring on the normally white underside and eye patch. Travelling with the whales on their daily rounds, we began to observe the strong social nature of the killer whale pod. Calves are usually seen just behind and to the side of their mothers, except at certain times of the day when they are allowed to roam within a few hundred yards or are taken care of by other mature whales. Older cows – aunts – often take the pod's calves to a quiet bay to play or fish.

The bulls usually stay out from shore, congregating together, indicating the pod's general direction and movement. Most bulls seem wary of our boat and any contact with man. The majority of our close encounters have been initiated by playful, curious juveniles – old enough to be free of their mothers but without an overdeveloped sense of caution.

The whales often rest together, lying on the surface for a minute and a half at five-minute intervals, for periods of up to four hours. Whales are voluntary breathers, unlike man, and must constantly 'wake themselves up' to surface and take oxygen during rest-time. The entire pod's breathing is virtually synchronized, though they are vocally silent during these periods. All our close-up film footage in 1973 and some in 1974 was taken during these resting periods when we paddled a canoe quietly among the pod as they lay on the surface.

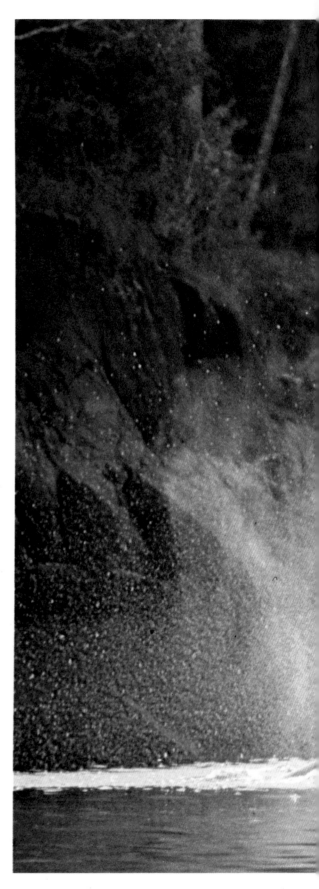

Cow and calf whales exhale in unison. The spray, backlit by the sun, hangs in the air even after they are gone

**Bull killer whale at rest. Though not strictly speaking an endangered species, the killer whale is wantonly shot by fishermen and others, partly from boredom, partly because of the animal's undeserved 'bad reputation'**

Also in 1973 and 1974, we swam with members of Stubbs's pod and another pod of eight whales called Hooker's pod (named after a mature bull with a forward-hooked dorsal fin over four feet high). The first time, in late July 1973, James Hunter and Graeme Ellis (biologist and former killer whale trainer) took turns lying on the surface of the water in a wet suit and snorkel while a single juvenile *orca* broke away from the pod and checked them out. The whale swam so close to Graeme Ellis that he was able to positively identify the young male's penile slit. The whale made repeated passes curiously eyeing each diver before returning to the pod. On later occasions, we obtained brief underwater footage of Stubbs's pod, including a sequence of a mother with her suckling calf.

In August and September 1975, Peter Vatcher, John Oliphant, and I spent a few weeks intensively photographing Stubbs's pod from a Zodiac rubber raft. We concentrated on two juveniles, nicknamed 'the twins' since they were always seen together. For a week of all-day sessions with Stubbs's pod, every time we motored in the vicinity, the twins swam over to the Zodiac and leaped out of the water around the boat like porpoises off the bow. Sometimes they would glide back and forth beneath our boat dragging strips of kelp like streamers clenched between their teeth. Other times, they paced us while we motored along, bobbing their heads and looking at us with their beady eyes. Every maneuver was accomplished with tremendous speed and facility (killer whales can reach estimated speeds of 30 mph); they frequently created complete havoc as the three of us tried to photograph them, tripping over each other in the process. Scenes like these could continue for half an hour before the twins would suddenly leave us and return to the rest of the pod.

In 1976 and 1977 Peter Vatcher and I again met up with the twins and Stubbs's pod. They seemed to recognize us – at least our Zodiac – and were once more uninhibited in their close approaches and eagerness to play. That playful nature, I think, is a vital aspect of a killer whale's personality. For us, of course, it is always exhilarating!

Killer whales are not endangered. They were never extensively hunted by whalers because of their small size. The Japanese and Norwegian small-whale fisheries may have depleted stocks along their own coasts since 1950; population studies need to be made. In any case, *orcas* are not part of the well known whale slaughter. Still, they *are* threatened by man's increased need for habitat, ocean resources, and entertainment.

Since 1962, 277 killer whales have been netted for the world's aquaria – exclusively from southern British Columbia and Puget Sound waters. Of these, sixty-four were removed or cropped. This regular cropping and a controversy over capture methods has recently led to protective measures for the 300 or so killer whales in B.C. and Washington State waters. Detailed population studies, begun in 1971 by Dr Michael Bigg of Canada's Fisheries Research Board, will determine long-term effects on this population, one of the few which are reasonably accessible for field studies in the wild. At least until the research is complete, permits to take *orcas* are restricted to replacing those already in Canadian aquaria. In Washington State whale captures have now ceased, but there is talk of opening up Alaska to supply the powerful *Sea World* chain of American aquaria. Conservationists in both countries are now lobbying for a complete ban on killer whale captures.

A little-publicized threat to killer whale numbers has been the wanton shooting of these animals in every ocean. The shootings stem from the killer whale's bad reputation – his voracious appetite – and the fear, hatred, or simple boredom of certain boaters and fishermen. I have seen these whale poachers in action off the Canadian coast; but the shootings are even more common elsewhere. A 1973 statistic revealed that sixty per cent of all killer whales caught and examined by scientists had bullet holes in their bodies.

Recently, killer whale shootings have declined, due to increased knowledge and public awareness of these fascinating marine mammals. Captive killer whales have helped reverse man's original view of them. We still call them 'killers', but it's man, of course – man alone – who deserves the title.

# BIRDS

## THE MAURITIUS KESTREL

David McKelvey

American author Mark Twain once described Mauritius as a heavenly sanctuary created by a beneficent Deity. Geologists argue that it is the remains of an ancient shield volcano, long dormant and eroded into a fantastic series of miniature mountain ranges, deep gorges, and verdant plains. Conservationists, however, sadly regard this most beautiful of the Indian Ocean Mascarene Islands as the home of the dodo, their synonym for extinction. Less well known than the ungainly dodo (but just as dead) are the large reddish-brown flightless land rail, the gray land rail, the red, white and blue Dutch pigeons, the Mauritius scops owl, the huge thick-billed ground parrot, and at least twenty other avian species. All these unique creatures disappeared shortly after the appearance of the first explorers with their monkeys, dogs, pigs, goats, and cats. All the remaining endemic species of land birds are threatened by the same forces that so successfully eliminated their fellow inhabitants.

Since conservationists, ornithologists, and aviculturalists have recently begun to have notable success in the manipulation of falcon populations, the interest in the pitifully small remnant population of Mauritius kestrels

(*Falco punctatus*) has been honed to a fine edge. This beautifully patterned, medium sized kestrel has a total distribution limited to the island of Mauritius. The total world population of thirteen individuals survives in a small area of degraded native forest in the south-west corner of the island.

Because of a number of factors working against its survival, the Mauritius kestrel is in a startlingly precarious position. Over 300 years ago, crab-eating macaque monkeys were introduced to the island by Portuguese sailors. This adaptable and omnivorous species was only too eager to add to its diet the eggs of any bird it encountered. Many endemic and indigenous species suffered, among them the lovely pink pigeon and the Mauritius ring-necked parrot, both of which species barely survive today. Over the years, Dutch, French, and English governments encouraged the growth of a highly profitable sugar industry, which has totally eliminated the lowland and lower slope native forests. The colonists introduced plant species, numbering in the hundreds, which have virtually choked the vestigial remains of the upland forests with an understorey that entirely inhibits natural regrowth of native plant species.

Some thirty-five endemic species of birds, several species of reptiles, and one species of bat occur now only as bones preserved from deposits in the marshes, or as poorly preserved museum skins and mounts. The various groups of colonists replaced such unusual species as the flightless red rail (a hen-sized vestigial winged forest rail), the blue Dutch pigeon, and a six-foot-tall moorhen, with various species from other lands. Indian mongooses and mynahs, Javan deer, Asian parakeets, African finches, English sparrows, Chinese doves, guineafowl, rats, mice, feral cats, feral pigs, feral dogs, feral goats – the list seems as endless as the damage they have done to the ecosystem.

It is a tribute to the adaptability of the

**Many interesting and unique birds have vanished from the beautiful Indian Ocean island of Mauritius since the arrival of the first explorers. The Mauritius kestrel is now almost symbolic of the fight for survival of the remaining endemic land birds**

kestrels that thirteen of them survive today, after three centuries of competition, predation, and habitat destruction. Due to agriculture, cyclonic activity, and re-afforestation projects, the native forest areas are steadily shrinking. This puts the kestrels in constant friction with the predatory crab-eating macaques, with an estimated population of 12,000 animals. The mynahs and Indian ring-neck parakeets compete with the kestrels for nest holes, as do the indigenous white-tailed tropic birds.

Of the three remaining pairs of kestrels living in the wild, two pairs have been able to select a safely inaccessible crevice on a basalt cliff-face in which to raise their young. The third pair has a tradition of using tree cavities for nest sites, resulting in a total lack of breeding success for the last five years.

The behavior and basic biology of these interesting little falcons is quite typical of kestrels the world over, with one notable exception. The Mauritius kestrel has evolved an almost hawk-like hunting technique. Consequently it shows a shorter, more rounded wing structure adapted for life below the forest canopy, where it makes its hunting forays after geckos, large insects, and the endemic species of white-eye. The typical kestrel soaring and hovering flight style is reserved for courtship and territorial displays. Except when it has to cross the narrow valleys in its precipitous habitat, the hunting kestrel slips quietly from tree to tree, landing near the main trunk and sitting quietly while scanning for prey.

Geckos are captured with incredibly swift dashes from a concealed position, as they sun themselves on tree limbs. At times the male and female kestrel will hunt in unison, one pushing the gecko, who runs to the other side of the tree into the range of the second kestrel's talons. Smaller birds, usually the endemic gray white-eye or the introduced common waxbill, are no match for the foraging kestrel. He employs the simple ruse of waiting for the prey to cross an open ravine, then pursues it and plucks it out of the air with the minimum of effort.

The large dragonflies and cicadas, which form the major portion of the insects consumed, present a more challenging target. The kestrels fly down wooded roads and pursue the nimble dragonflies, hunting them in the protected openings up into the sky, where a truly skilled show of acrobatic flying is necessary to bag the quarry. Cicadas are picked from the forest canopy with the kestrel occasionally hanging inverted from bunches of leaves as he seizes these large juicy green insects.

The breeding season commences in September, with the noisy aerial courtship and declamation of territory of the kestrel pair. Each morning at dawn the male rises into the pale sky, screaming 'kree-kree-kree-kree' in sequences of four. He begins to soar in circles, alternating his soaring with a rapid shallow flapping of wings. When the female joins him, they frequently make spectacular stoops at each other, rolling and plunging, first above and then below the crag where they have decided to nest.

The male will begin to explore the air bubble holes left in the lava when it cooled centuries ago. These bubbles range in size from that of a football to several feet in circumference. If carefully selected, one can provide a safe, dry, roomy site in which to rear the two to four young. Unfortunately, the indigenous white-tailed tropic bird, a large, aggressive, gull-like seabird with a distinctive, long, pointed tail, often selects the same hole as does a pair of kestrels. This results in a no-contest ownership on the part of the heavy-billed tropic bird. Indian mynahs and feral pigeons will, at times, occupy holes suitable for kestrels and, by sheer perseverance and superior numbers, discourage the kestrels.

When the male finds an untenanted hole of suitable dimensions, he enters it in a hunched-shouldered posture and calls 'kek! kek! kek!' If the female enters, they will stand hunched over with their tails fanned and 'kek! kek!' at each other. Soon the male will begin to lie down and make scraping and pushing motions to define a bowl-like depression in the gravel and detritus accumulated in the hole. If the female is sufficiently stimulated by the male's displays and the nest site, she also will begin to scrape and call a staccatto 'kikkikit!'

All the holes on the cliff-face will be examined, at least by the male, and much abortive scraping and 'kiking' will occur until the female indicates by her behavior that a proper site is chosen.

The male begins to feed the female on portions of his prey, possibly to allow her system to devote its metabolism to egg production instead of hunting. Indeed, the male is such a tireless provider that the female has a

Tamarin escarpment, where there is a basalt-cliff nesting site for one pair of the rare kestrels. This nest hole appears to be 'monkey-proof' and young birds were successfully reared there in 1976

much greater supply of prey, in the form of geckos, finches, and white-eyes, than she could possibly consume. Even when not hunting, the male retains a lizard or a portion of a small bird in his talons as he flies back and forth across the cliff-face, hoping to tempt the female to fly out and take it from his talons.

As soon as the female is receptive, the male initiates copulation at every possible opportunity. The first clutch of two to four reddish-brown eggs, speckled with darker brown at the larger end, is deposited directly into the scrape made by the parents. No nesting material is carried into the cavity by the parent birds. Feathers and bones of the prey carried into the nest hole may accidentally be incorporated into the nest scrape, as may molted plumage of the adults. Incubation begins with the first egg and is carried out entirely by the female. Twenty-four hours elapse between eggs in the production of the rest of the clutch. Although the male will enter the nest hole during the brief absence of the female, I do not believe he contributes significantly to any real incubation.

The period of incubation lasts for twenty-eight days, with the embryo first puncturing the shell on the twenty-sixth day, and emerging on the twenty-eighth. The young kestrels hatch twenty-four hours apart. The tiny young are clothed in soft white down. Their eyes are closed and the mandibles and toenails are of pale horn colour. Their first vocalizations are a thin peeping, reminiscent of those of a young domestic pigeon.

Within just two hours of hatching, the female offers small morsels of flesh to her young. The young bird raises its head and makes pecking motions as the female holds her meat-laden bill next to its beak. Upon contact with the meat, the young kestrel vigorously swallows whatever morsels it can take into its bill. Food is offered at hourly intervals during daylight hours and is usually accepted. The surplus food not passing into the digestive tract is stored as a protruding ball in the crop at the base of the neck.

Young birds of prey grow with phenomenal speed, and the Mauritius kestrel is no exception. At three days of age the eyes open and the movements become co-ordinated in reaching for food. At two weeks the young can stand; they are now covered in woolly gray down tufted with wisps of the natal down. At three weeks, the primary, scapular, and tail plumage have emerged. At five weeks the body is well feathered, only the crown of the head remaining downy. At this stage the young can walk and are playing about with pieces of prey that they are now able to tear apart and devour. The female now helps the male with the hunting to supply the ravenous demands of the young. Loud calling is now heard, and the young are busy strengthening their wing muscles when not sleeping or eating.

Between the seventh and eighth weeks, the young cling to the opening of the nest site and beat their nearly full grown wings, even letting go and scrambling over the adjacent rocks before popping back into the safety of the nest. At this time the young are near-replicas of their parents, with shorter wings and tail. The legs and bare skin of the face are grayish yellow, unlike the bright yellow of the adults. Learning to fly is not a problem with the kestrels. Instinct and abundant energy provide the stimulus, and the buoyant cliffside air currents lift the eager falcons over the valley. Within hours, soaring and turning are perfected, while only poor landings and stumbling re-entry to the nest demonstrate the novice status of the now fully airborne kestrels.

The parents return about every two hours bearing prey that they deliver to the nest site or to the most demonstratively screaming young one. The harassed parents often drop a lizard or a wounded bird on the rocks near a screaming fledgling, which then grabs it in its talons and eats it, shielding its meal with spread wings and tail from less fortunate siblings.

There is a stage when the parents actually seem to fear the aggressive, demanding young, and they then deliver the prey to a nearby ledge or drop it out of the air to be captured by the pursuing young on the wing. With the superabundance of food species in the area, the young naturally begin to make attempts to feed themselves, with varying degrees of success. The parents' visits with food slow down to twice a day after about the tenth week, and the hungry young have semi-starvation as an impetus to their efforts. Only a physically or mentally defective young bird could fail to find sufficient food among the warm tropical forests and gorges of Mauritius. By the twelfth or fourteenth week, the young are independent of the parents, who are now molting their primaries and tails.

On fine warm mornings the whole family will soar briefly over the roosting cliff, the young sporting about with all the vigor of youth, while the ragged outline of the parents' molting wings clearly shows the age difference. Unlike many other falcon species, the Mauritius kestrels continue to frequent the territory of their parents for one full year, co-existing in a peaceful manner. With suitable habitat at a premium and food abundant, this is perhaps an insular adaptation to a once high population density.

The following September, the adult male kestrel disperses his remaining young with gradually intensifying hostility until they fear for their safety if they do not remain well out on the periphery of the home range. Quite spectacular flying contests occur between adults and young, accompanied by much diving, stooping, and screaming, but always the young lose out and must disperse as the next breeding cycle is about to begin.

The life history outlined above now occurs all too infrequently for the remaining eleven wild Mauritius kestrels. The last young were fledged on 3 and 7 December 1976; before that two years had elapsed between successful nestings. Two of the five young fledged were offspring of a pair of siblings hatched two years previously. All five young were fledged from holes in high basalt and tuff cliffs, unreachable by monkeys.

Captive breeding has proven to be a valuable technique for the management of endangered falcon species. Its object is the release of the resulting young in the wild at sites suitable for their continued survival. Cornell University in the United States has pioneered in this field, with the peregrine falcon, with some very promising results. The World Wildlife Fund, in cooperation with the International Council for Bird Preservation and the New York Zoological Society, decided in 1973 to undertake a project to staff and fund a captive breeding project and habitat management scheme for the Mauritius kestrel on its home island.

With the permission of the Forestry Department of Mauritius, a pair of kestrels who had a non-productive tradition of nesting in trees were taken into captivity early in 1974 and placed in specially built aviaries in the gardens of a private aviculturalist. The kestrels settled down to their captive condition with remarkable ease and within six months had mated and produced three eggs. These eggs were transferred to an electric incubator where two proved to be fertile, and after the twenty-eight-day incubation period, one kestrel successfully hatched. The other egg ceased development approximately one week prior to hatching.

Skilled personnel kept a round-the-clock vigil over the infant kestrel, providing it with morsels of day-old chicken, lizard, and mouse. The kestrel grew with normal speed and health until it reached twenty-one days of age. Sadly, one of the all-too-frequent electric power failures common on Mauritius ultimately caused the demise of this rarest of young falcons. The surge of power back into the lines damaged the thermostatic apparatus and simply and quickly overheated the kestrel, causing his death.

Bad luck has plagued this pair of kestrels ever since. In 1975, fertile eggs were destroyed by a mentally disturbed person who gained access to the guarded grounds at night. A second clutch of three eggs was laid. The one fertile egg hatched, but the young one was apparently cannibalized by its mother. In 1976, the Mauritius Government assumed responsibility for the housing of the project, and the kestrels were moved to a new aviary site. The constant activity and noises, related to continued construction of the endangered species breeding center, apparently disturbed them to the point where they produced only one, infertile egg. The pair of kestrels appeared to

**There are only about a dozen Mauritius kestrels, which makes it about the rarest bird of prey in the world. The World Wildlife Fund is involved in a captive breeding project on the island, which it is hoped will ensure the species' survival. Survival of the kestrel in the wild, however, will probably depend on the creation of refuges, removal of monkeys, and provision of a warden to ensure the safety of nesting pairs**

be in excellent health, with copulation occurring many times each day. The female was eager to incubate her egg, but infertility prevented any successful results.

The remaining three pairs in the wild had better luck in 1976. Pair number one, at the Bel-ombre cliff, at last chose a rock opening that was monkey-proof and were able to fledge three fine young and keep them to independence. Pair number two, at the Tamarin escarpment, produced two youngsters. Despite one fledging prematurely, they were able to keep and rear both of their young. (Pair number two are the 1973 young of pair number one.) The remaining pair of kestrels, that had for years been loyal to an unsuccessful tree nest site, have turned to roosting and inhabiting a fine series of sheer rock faces in Brise-fer mountain. With a bit of luck the two pairs will nest again in their safe sites and the third pair will at last tenant a cliff hole.

All five young reared in 1976 are still to be seen scattered in the few square miles of habitat left to them. Encouraging news is all too precious where rare species are concerned. Although the wild kestrels have shown a recent increase, it is doubtful whether the species can survive without the creation of refuges, the removal of monkeys, and a special warden provided to ensure the safety of nesting pairs.

The recent interest shown by the Government of Mauritius in developing a captive breeding center, where they have several Rodrigues fruit bats, pink pigeons, and a pair of kestrels, is indeed laudable. Success is now being achieved in rearing pink pigeons in captivity, and they hope for success with the echo parakeet and the fruit bats. We can only hope that soon a program of habitat restoration, refuge development, and wardening will allow the kestrel and other endangered endemic species to continue as an integral part of their fragile ecosystem, as well as fascinating cage birds.

# THE BALD EAGLE

Malcolm Penny

'I wish that the Bald Eagle had not been chosen as the representative of our country; he is a bird of bad moral character; he does not get his living honestly; he is generally poor and very lousy.' (Benjamin Franklin, 1784).

It seems a pity, really, that more rural Americans don't accept Ben Franklin's account of their national bird's 'bad moral character'. He was referring to the fact that, far from being a great and glorious hunter, the bald eagle is primarily a scavenger of dead and dying fish, and a pirate, chasing ospreys until they are terrified into dropping their catch. But such is the ancient tradition of eagles as heroic killers that many people, sheep-farmers in particular, still regard them as major predators, and shoot them whenever they get the chance. It is a bitter fact that the chief cause of death among bald eagles in North America is still shooting, even after years of protective legislation and educational press releases.

In the worst recorded episode, in Wyoming in 1970–71, an investigation of some cases of illegal poisoning of eagles led the United States Fish and Wildlife Service further than they could have imagined, into very murky regions. During the questioning of one of the suspects in the poisoning case, they heard of a group of farmers who were in the habit of chartering helicopters to go out shooting eagles from the air. It was soon established that at least 770 eagles, both golden and bald, had been shot from one helicopter in twelve months; and there were other hunters at work too.

Before we condemn the Wyoming hunters as callous murderers, it might be valuable to look at the background of the story. Although it is history now, and people's attitudes have changed to some degree, the underlying mis-understanding is still there, and ought to be identified.

The story is a complex one, which began a long time ago with the opening up of the Prairie States as sheep pastures. Overstocking and erratic rainfall led to a rapid deterioration in the grasslands, followed by an invasion of shrubs, and a marked change in what had been a uniform and relatively stable ecosystem. As the shrubs grew, they provided shelter and food for a vastly increased population of prairie dogs and rabbits, animals which had always existed in the original habitat, but never in such numbers until it was altered to suit them. This in its turn led to an increase in the numbers of golden (and, to a lesser extent, bald) eagles, which ventured on to the plains to prey on the small mammals. So far, so ecological.

Meanwhile, the sheep were doing less and less well, with dreadful mortality at lambing time; and no eagle, least of all a bald eagle, is too proud to scavenge a recently expired lamb. Depressed farmers, riding through their under-fed and diseased flocks, would have seen eagles on corpses – and up sprang the old myths of the feathered killers, and with the myths, the gun barrels.

Still holding off from the lynching party, we must consider another factor which makes it easier at least to understand how the farmers' bloodlust was roused as it must have been. The Agriculture Department in the United States pays compensation to farmers whose stock is depleted by predators, presumably as a measure to prevent the farmers taking the law into their own hands, and trying to wipe out the predators with poisons which will endanger other forms of life. However, there is no compensation payable for beasts which die in droughts or as a result of overstocking. What could be more natural, then, than the farmers shifting some of the blame for their losses away from their own bad luck or bad management, and getting some money back at the same time, by blaming predators? The coyote came in for some of the blame, and the eagles took the rest. The result was that the published figures – official government figures, but derived directly from the farmers' exaggerated, not to say fictitious, returns – announced each year that compensation had been paid on so many sheep and lambs killed by predators. In 1970 a total of 8,600 deaths were credited to eagles alone. To the farmers it

Though it has been well known for hundreds of years that the bald eagle is primarily a scavenger of dead and dying fish, the main enemies of America's national bird today are still men with guns, who believe that the eagle is a major predator of sheep

must have seemed incontrovertible evidence.

Around this time there were several independent surveys of the causes of lamb mortality. Thousands of carcasses were autopsied in half-a-dozen states, and the prime cause of death was found to be a combination of malnutrition and parasitic infestation. In one or two cases the researchers were uncertain whether an eagle had actually hastened the end of a moribund lamb – nearly all the corpses had of course been eaten by the birds – and in one exceptional case an eagle was actually seen on a lamb which was still alive. To underline the exception, it was an adult bald eagle, primarily a waterside scavenger, which was involved. It surely must have believed that the lamb was dead. There was no other confirmed record of any eagle attacking a live animal.

The authorities seem to have been slow to accept this evidence, because for a time permits were issued to farmers to shoot golden eagles in defense of their stock at certain times of year. Bald eagles were already totaly protected; but the juvenile bald is so similar to a golden eagle in the air or at a distance that most ornithologists won't commit themselves to an identification, so of course balds were shot as well. Partly because of this, in 1969 the Department of the Interior stopped issuing licenses to shoot eagles at all, except in cases so strictly defined that no one could qualify.

To turn once more to the accused in the dock, we can see much more of their point of view. Given government statistics which showed as plain as a prairie moon that eagles were killing stock, and in large numbers, and effectively denied the right legally to do anything about it, some of them were almost bound to reach for their guns, and make sure that they used them to the best effect. One rancher paid a helicopter team $15,000 in bounties for predators shot on his land, at the rate of $50 per coyote, and $25 per eagle.

The case became a national news story, and when the defendants were found guilty, and then fined a few hundred dollars and sent home, the outcry from conservationists was loud and long. Similar events in other states at about the same time attracted less notice than the first story, but the local noises were just as loud. The cry was always to increase the protection of eagles by enforcing harsher penalties for killing them. But it is of course a truism that protection will achieve nothing

unless it is backed by public understanding of the facts. The only good to come out of the case might be a slowly dawning realization by the farmers that the eagle is not to blame; but until they know that for certain, the risk of a $500 fine won't stop them. One can hardly resist adding that if half the energy spent on blackening the hunters in the national press had been devoted to explaining to them and their neighbors the details of how they arrived in their present fix, more lasting good would have been done. I repeat the sad fact that the most frequent cause of death to bald eagles now, several years after Wyoming, is shooting.

On the more positive side, many causes of death or breeding failure are being identified and eliminated or reduced. The mortality caused by the use of organochlorines (DDT, DDE, PCBs, and dieldrin, and their relations), whether as pesticides or as industrial chemicals, is ultimately controllable by restrictions on their use, and some spectacular results have come in a short time. In the Chesapeake Bay area, near Washington, DC, breeding success has risen among one group of nests by twenty-five per cent in two years. Admittedly, this marks the beginning of a recovery from a very

**An eagle's nest in the Florida Keys (left). Despite protection, the eagles do not flourish alongside the burgeoning waterborne sports, such as fishing, boating, and water-skiing. Two young eagles (above) in an Alaskan nest. Though only 700 or so pairs are breeding in the lower forty-eight states, the estimate for Alaska is ten times as great**

low point, but it is a beginning, and it can only continue to improve as the use of the chemicals is more carefully controlled.

An unexpected beam of light in the eagles' darkness came from the work of a falconer from Boise, Idaho. Morlan Nelson was already famous, a colorful figure with his trained eagles and peregrines, when the Utah Power and Light Utility approached him to help solve an awkward problem. Five hundred eagles had been found electrocuted at the foot of power poles in four years, and people (Nelson not the quietest among them) were beginning to make rude noises in the press. To the Power Company, it was largely a public relations exercise, but to Nelson it was a chance to try to reduce the pressure on his beloved eagles, so he accepted. He trained one of his eagles (a young golden) to fly to dummy power poles which he erected in his back garden, and he filmed it with a high-speed cine-camera as it landed and took off. He then analyzed the film to find exactly when and how the eagles were short-circuiting the wires and dying.

His results showed that there was a simple modification which could be made to most existing designs of power pole, to make the separation between the wires larger than the eagle's wingspan in its typical landing posture; and second, that one of the most common causes of death was the eagle making contact between one of the conductors and the lightning conductor on the pole, effectively earthing the power supply through its body. The answer was so simple and cheap that it amounted to genius: cut the lightning conductor and bend it to leave a three-inch gap, small enough for a lightning flash to jump, but too wide to carry a spark if an eagle spread itself across to the conductor from a cable. It was not even necessary to make the modification to every pole: Nelson's experience enabled him to say which poles in a row would be used as feeding and hunting perches by eagles, and which would not. While he was at it, he designed a safe nesting platform which could be attached to the poles while the engineers were increasing the cable separation.

The Power Company did as he suggested, and reaped the benefit of the wise expenditure of some thousands of dollars by seeing their actions acclaimed across the nation. Others have followed suit; indeed, they have gone further. Eagles often nest on steel pylons, and

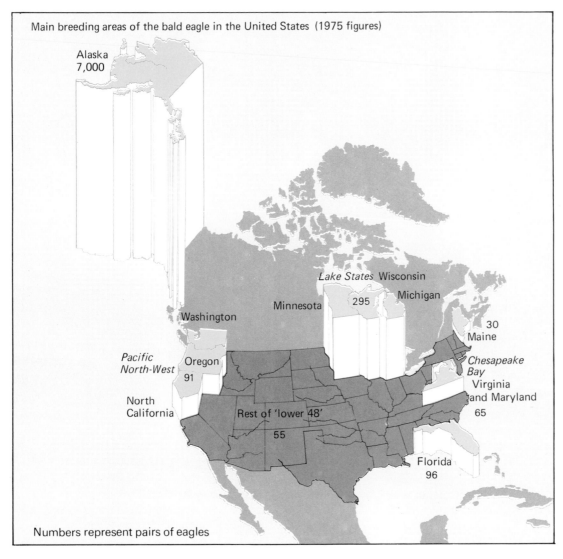

Main breeding areas of the bald eagle in the United States (1975 figures)

Alaska
7,000

Lake States Wisconsin
Minnesota
295
Michigan

30
Maine

Washington

Pacific
North-West
Oregon
91

Chesapeake
Bay
Virginia
and Maryland
65

North
California

Rest of 'lower 48'
55

Florida
96

Numbers represent pairs of eagles

their ragged piles of sticks can get blown on to one of the cables. The result is usually a short fire, and the death of the young in the nest. In the recent past, engineers would climb the pylons with insulated poles to push the nests off; but now they carry small saws instead, to trim the overhanging twigs and make the nest safe. There is a change of heart among the American people, even among a supposedly hard-bitten lot like the Power Companies. Public relations, a much maligned exercise, reflects the changing wishes and preferences of the public after all.

Research on eagles has never been easy with wild birds, because of their timidity and the remoteness of their nesting grounds, but the research has to be done if conservation plans are to be founded anywhere near fact. Some ingenious work by Dr Thomas Dunstan in Minnesota succeeded in tracing the route taken by birds from the Lakes States to their wintering grounds. He launched dead pike on to the surface of a lake, each one 'bugged' with a tiny radio transmitter, and waited for eagles to pick them up and take them back to their nests. Then, using a directional radio antenna, he could locate the nest by picking up the bleeps from the fish. Climbing to the nest, he removed any well grown chicks, attached a micro-miniaturized transmitter to them by means of his own special harness, and put them back. Then it became relatively simple to track them across country by car and light aircraft when they fledged and flew. By establishing the routes they take, and how far they travel, and most importantly where their staging posts are,

**Research on wild bald eagles has never been easy, but one researcher fitted dead pike with tiny radio bugs; this enabled him to locate the eagles' nests, and in due course to fit radio transmitters to the young birds. In this way he has identified their routes and staging posts during their travels**

**(Over page) This eagle, just starting to develop its white head, is an immature bird. But already it has the famed hooked bill that is the cause of its reputation as a fearsome predator**

Dunstan has identified many of the key sites which must be protected at certain times of year.

One such place is Glacier, Montana, where a spectacular convocation of eagles (the correct term, and very fitting) gathers each fall to feed on salmon dying after their breeding run upriver. The wintering ground is well protected, though waters round about are pretty heavily shot over for duck. During routine biopsies of his eagles, Dunstan discovered that they were heavily dosed with DDT, a surprizing result since the fish both on their breeding grounds and at Glacier are relatively clean. By collecting and X-raying regurgitated pellets from under the roosting trees, he found that they had been feeding not on fish, but on ducks which had been wounded or killed by the hunters and not picked up. (American hunters seldom use dogs for fear one of their

colleagues will shoot them.) It was easy to show that the ducks came from agricultural areas some distance away, where the rivers were liberally laced with run-off pesticides. A bald eagle cannot catch a healthy duck, but here was a ready-made food supply, with the added bonus of lead poisoning or DDT poisoning, or both. Sometimes it seems as if the poor eagles just can't win.

That impression is reinforced by a visit to Florida. After Alaska, Florida used to be the bald eagle's great stronghold, but now it has become the Real Estate capital of America. Apart from the carefully guarded Everglades National Park, which is the home of a few pairs, the rest of Florida seems to be losing its wild quality and its eagles at an alarming rate. The osprey is still quite common, but it can fish unmolested by eagles, because there are hardly any left. Part of this is due to the builders and town 'unplanners' – though, to be fair, some of them are actually protecting eagle nests on building sites in the (probably vain) hope that the birds will come back when it's all over – but the larger part follows from the vast increase in waterborne sport, fishing, water-skiing, yachting, and the like. I flew over the Florida Keys, once silent unspoiled mangrove islets, spotting eagle nests from a light aircraft with a park biologist, while we were making the 'Survival' film about the bald eagle: the most depressing thing to see there is the mass of criss-cross boat tracks in the turtle grass, scars from the propellers of hundreds of small craft. There must be a colossal traffic there at weekends. Many of the Keys have eagle nests on them, but only a few are active now.

So do we write off the American eagle, to be no more real to the next but one generation of Americans than the unicorn on the British Royal Coat of Arms? I think not, on the whole. The pressure of research on the one hand, and the changing attitude and receptiveness of the Americans at large on the other, makes it more likely than not that it will survive. Bald eagles have been bred in captivity at the Patuxent Wildlife Research Center in Maryland, and other research there shows evidence of a gradual drop in the amount of pesticide pollution in some areas. The plan is to release 'clean' eagles into a cleaner environment in due course. An experimental 'transplant' of eggs from (clean) Minnesota to (dirty)

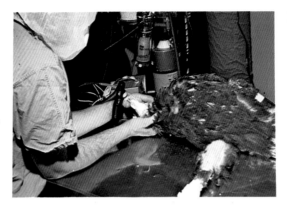

Maine met with a lot of opposition from scientists, and was not an unqualified success, but enough was learned to show that with proper precautions wild eagles will adopt strange eggs, and even chicks.

Although the latest estimate finds only 708 pairs of bald eagles breeding in the forty-eight contiguous states, the estimate for Alaska is at least 7,000 pairs, and there are more in Canada, so that the species itself is fairly secure. It is now up to each state to find out what has been killing its eagles, and set about putting things to rights. Even where the eagle is extinct – and once it bred in all the states (except Hawaii) – the environment could at least be cleaned up ready for the time when transplanting has been perfected.

There is one more anecdote in the bald eagle story. In the course of making the 'Survival' program, we followed Tom Dunstan to Minnesota to film him radio-marking and tracking an eagle. I had a letter from him six months later, to say that he had seen 'our' bird again: it was in a parcel delivered to his home in Idaho from a friend in Montana. The bird had been shot dead with a rifle.

Which brings us back to where we started. For all the legislation and research, there is still a long way to go before the bald eagle can be said to be safe, and the route is the long uphill trail called education.

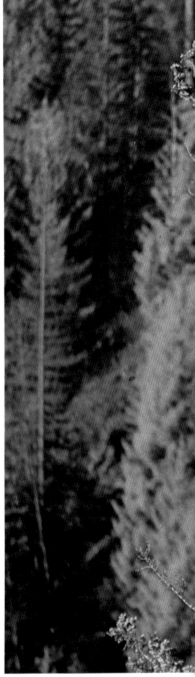

An operation on the leg of an injured bald eagle (left). Some birds are being bred at the Patuxent Wildlife Research Center in Maryland where a wide range of scientific research into the species is being carried out.

Spectacular gatherings of bald eagles can be seen in Glacier National Park, Montana, each fall (above). The birds come to feed on the dying salmon which have just finished their breeding run upriver. Unfortunately for the eagles they also feed on ducks which have been shot but not collected by hunters. It was found that many of these ducks were heavily contaminated with DDT—and lead from gunshot

# THE GIANT GREBE OF GUATEMALA

Anne LaBastille

A huge tropical moon silhouetted the volcanic cones of Atitlán, Tolimán, and San Pedro upon the shimmering surface of Lake Atitlán. Slowly, I steered my boat towards a bed of reeds which rustled softly in the night breeze. Out of the black mass came the challenging call of a giant pied-billed grebe – 'caow, caow, caow, caow-uhh, caow-uhh, caow-uhh'.

Cutting off my outboard engine, I switched on a portable tape recorder and answered my quarry with an exact imitation of his territorial call. The response was instant. Thus, by sound, I canvassed the steep and rocky shoreline of this deep highland lake. For three nights I continued this census in order to obtain an accurate count of this grebe's dwindling numbers. When I finished one dawn morning in 1965, I had counted fewer than eighty birds.

I was counting one of the rarest and most endangered waterbirds in the Western Hemisphere. This species of grebe (*Podilymbus gigas*) occurs nowhere else on earth. The giant pied-billed grebe is endemic to mile-high Lake Atitlán; just as two other close relatives, the short-winged grebe (*Centropelma micropterus*) and the puna grebe (*Podiceps taczanowskii*), live only on Lake Titicaca, Bolivia, and Lake Junín, Peru, respectively. All three are flightless and can barely walk on land. However, the Atitlán grebe is a superb diver and a veritable submarine beneath the water.

Formerly the population of these grebes was a stable 200 or more individuals, as first reported by ornithologists Alexander Wetmore and Ludlow Griscom, who visited Lake Atitlán almost fifty years ago. My own first census in 1960 confirmed this number. Later, my calculations of the carrying capacity of this habitat put the figure more precisely at 280

birds. Apparently the grebes had prospered for centuries, living on this 400-meter-deep lake without visible outlets and landlocked by escarpments and volcanoes which reach almost 4,000 meters high. The thick shoreline fringe of reeds and cattails offered protection from predators and good roosting and nesting sites. The native fisheries of small minnows and freshwater crabs evidently provided sufficient food sources. Despite their physical inability to migrate or leave the lake, the grebes had probably stayed in sound balance with the environment.

Don Emilio Crespo, at eighty-seven years one of the lake's oldest residents, reminisced to me: 'Yes, the *zambullidores* [bird which dives] were all around the lake when I was young. I could hardly sleep on full moon nights with their calling.'

The giant pied-bill is a handsome gray-black waterbird with neat white eye-rings and a heavy ivory-colored bill circled by a black ring, or pied-mark. It looks like the common pied-bill of North America except that the Atitlán species grows twice as large. An adult Atitlán male weighs about two pounds; a common, one pound or less. The beak is stronger and larger in the former species. Its wings, however, still measure nearly the same length as, and have almost the same wing-loading as those of the smaller species. This means the larger grebe must support twice the weight per unit of wing area. Clearly, a problem in aerodynamics! Hence the giant grebe cannot fly.

How did this happen? Dr Alexander Wetmore, the world-renowned ornithologist, estimates that it took as long as 8,000 to 10,000 years for this once-migratory grebe to evolve into a large, flightless freak. During the cold epochs of the Ice Age, lakes in North America froze and the waterbirds were driven south. Lake Atitlán, deep, high, close to the Pacific Ocean, and only fourteen degrees from the equator, certainly remained open. Here, Dr Wetmore suggests, the grebes found conditions so favorable that they stayed and gradually lost their migratory urge. Slowly evolution worked its strange adaptations through genetics. Eventually, grebes became isolated 'Ice Age relics'.

As flying expertise was lost, the Atitlán grebe compensated by developing aquatic skills to an almost uncanny degree. It can regulate the air in its body to float at any depth,

**An adult male Lake Atitlán or giant pied-billed grebe. Confined to a single lake in Guatemala, it is one of the rarest waterbirds in the world. Saved from extinction once, it is still not, and perhaps never will be, secure**

swim underwater or long distances, emerge like a periscope with only eyes and beak out of the water, and submerge so quickly that legend says it can duck a hunter's shots. Legends also relate that the grebe can stay underwater for half an hour, and travel submerged for half a mile! I was sceptical. By timing and measuring countless dives, I learned that the bird seldom stays down longer than ninety seconds. And it usually moves no more than 100 meters underwater in one breathing space. Yet, the Atitlán grebe, when pressed, can swim submerged at almost five miles per hour. Its extremely caudal (rear) legs and large lobed feet (the three front toes of all grebes, coots, finfoots, and phalaropes are edged with lobed membranes) help give the bird added thrust in the water.

I kept hearing one folktale over and over again in my interviews with local people. It told how a grebe will commit suicide by diving down to a waterweed and hanging on until it drowns itself. 'If a *poc* [the local Mayan Indian name for the grebe] knows you are waiting for him with a shotgun or slingshot,' explained a Guatemalan fisherman seriously to me, 'it will just kill itself.'

Of course it wasn't true, but the grebes had good cause to commit suicide in the early 1960s. From 1960 to 1964, I watched environmental conditions grow worse and worse at Lake Atitlán. Then in 1964, I began a thorough ecological investigation to see what the trouble was. Soon the culprit appeared. I found that in 1958 and again in 1960, largemouth bass and crappies had been introduced into Lake Atitlán to improve sport fishing. No tests or controlled experiments were run. These exotic fish underwent a population explosion that deranged Atitlán's entire aquatic ecosystem. The voracious bass were devouring the small native fish, fresh-water crabs, frogs, and insects. They grew fat and cheeky. Some specimens weighed up to fifteen pounds! The sequences of this unwise introduction to a tropical lake were incredible.

Bass, being carnivorous fish, are notorious predators of aquatic life, including young waterbirds. They have been known on occasion to snatch warblers, red-wing blackbirds, and swallows that swoop too close to the water. They can also devour young ducks and geese. There was little doubt in my mind that the big bass in Lake Atitlán would take baby grebes. Moreover, juvenile grebes were hard-pressed

to find food because the bass were preying heavily on the original populations of fish and crabs which are the mainstay of a grebe's diet. Even the adult grebes were bothered by this unexpected competition.

The local Mayan Indians of the lake likewise were affected by the impoverishment of their fisheries. For centuries, the chief source of protein was the several species of tiny fish which were caught in special 'corrals', in wicker traps, and by spear. Once a fisherman could count on getting ten to twenty pounds, maybe more, of fish per day. These were dried and made into fish paste and fish stews. The crabs were caught at night by the light of flaming torches. Six dozen were an average night's catch. The crabs were popular in soups. But in the 1960s, fish catches dropped to two to four pounds per day, and crabs to one or two dozen. Most Indians are too poor to afford the proper tackle to take big bass. They do not know how to swim, hence they cannot use diving gear and spearguns. In effect, the new fish populations of bass and crappie were virtually untouchable save for a few young fish which fell to simple hooks and lines. The Indians began to experience protein deficiency and related illnesses. Waterbird poaching, therefore, rose in an effort to bring more meat back to their sparse diets.

Just five years after the bass introduction, I discovered that the *poc* population had tumbled from between 200 to 300 birds to about eighty – a sixty-eight per cent decrease. It seemed inevitable to me that the giant pied-billed grebe would follow the path of the passenger pigeon and great auk into oblivion. The species had, at best, five to ten years.

Determined to make a last-ditch stand to save the species from extinction, I conceived a four-point plan called 'Operation Protection of the Poc'. I believed that ten thousand years of evolution simply should not be wiped out by just a few months of human mismanagement. As Sir Peter Scott has said so eloquently, 'only natural cataclysmic forces have the right to take lives or force into extinction any wild creature.' So in 1965 and again in 1966 I obtained grants from the World Wildlife Fund, Smithsonian Institution, International Council for Bird Preservation, and National Geographic Society for field research and a conservation program. With this welcome aid, I was able to approach the Guatemalan Ministry

San Pedro's volcanic cone is one of three that overlook mile-high Lake Atitlán. The lake's very beauty may lead to ecological problems as mushrooming shoreline development—hotels and vacation homes—sweeps round the lake. A grebe's nest (right) in a cattail stand contains two fairly fresh eggs

of Agriculture, obtain the support of Jorge Ibarra, director of Guatemala's Museum of Natural History, and launch a cooperative campaign.

As the most immediate task, the ministry installed the very first game warden and patrol boat on Lake Atitlán. Three honorary wardens, including myself, were also appointed. Dressed in our new khaki-green uniforms with yellow-and-black *poc* emblems, we visited the twelve villages around the lake. Most of the lake's 50,000 Cakchiquel and Tzutuhil Indians live here. We met mayors, teachers, school children, and young men to whom we explained our mission.

I was especially anxious to involve these taciturn Indians in our conservation campaign since they habitually regard animals as sources of food or feathers. If they could be convinced that the birds were worth more alive than dead, our preservation program might succeed. Our psychology was to give the local people double incentives – money and pride. We explained that the bird was a tourist attraction and tourists brought money. Furthermore, that the Atitlán grebe existed nowhere else but in Guatemala, hence it was a rare resource worthy of great national concern and pride.

In each village, Guatemala's chief of wildlife introduced the new warden and warned that poachers would be prosecuted. He also advised that the shoreline vegetation could no longer be cut during the grebes' critical spring nesting season. Fortunately, two presidential decrees have provided legal backing. One prohibits the hunting of waterbirds on Lake Atitlán; the other curtails cutting reeds between 1 May and 15 August each year. In this way, native reed cutters will not disturb the nest or nest sites when the grebes need them most. However, since the Indians rely on a cottage industry of reed weaving to supply sleeping mats and little seats, the rest of the year is leniently left open to harvesting. Every reed cutter must cut only half his plot at one time and protect any birds or eggs he encounters. By good luck, this conservation law also helped improve the growth of the reed beds.

Our visits and warnings were just in time. It was early April and the grebes were beginning their reproductive season. Every day I spent hours in my boat recording their courtship displays and nesting ceremonies which had never before been described to science.

To my wonderment, I saw that male adult grebes announce their amorous moods with a resonant bellow – 'caow, caow, caow-uh'. This weird, gulping, territorial call is each male's way of defending its territory, usually a stretch of seventy to 140 meters within a reed bed. If another grebe should trespass, the owner goes into a frightening aggressive display which I named the 'snakehead display'. The affronted male swims at the intruder with his body half-submerged, his powerful feet kicking back a wake like an angry black torpedo. A broad ripple precedes him like a miniature tidal wave. As the bird nears his target, he floats higher, his neck crooks, feathers lift until the head looks almost twice as large, and the black-bibbed throat swells like the neck of a cobra. As one visiting birdwatcher exclaimed, 'he looks just like a pirate warship coming into firing range.'

If the trespasser insists on crossing the invisible line forming the boundary through the reeds, he is challenged to a fight. The two pivot around each other, bridling face-to-face. Suddenly, they rise out of the water and beat their little wings, then slash viciously at each other's heads and necks. After three or four minutes of battle, one usually retreats hastily. The victor, invariably, is the home-owner. He swims slowly back to the center of his territory, kicking water back in spurts as if to say, 'I showed you!'.

When male grebes are not braying out their call or fighting, they are busy with their mates. My impression is that grebes mate for life, or at least several years. Their courtship is one of grace and attentiveness. The pair may be feeding some ten meters apart. At an imperceptible signal, they hunch down and start swimming towards one another. Heads and bodies strain forward. In the instant before collision, they veer sideways, warble cozily in duet, and swim off side by side.

I became so enthusiastic about these original observations of grebe breeding behavior that I continued eagerly throughout the period of nesting, incubation, and raising the young. How often I echoed the words of the ornithologist Dr Arthur A. Allen: 'Few birds offer greater difficulties to the ornithologist who would become familiar with their lives.' Indeed! My trials included sunstroke, the sinking of my small boat in a storm, several mechanical failures of the motor, skin rashes from dragging

myself through the reed beds and mud, and amoebic dysentery.

Most of the time I was shut out by some of the densest stands of reeds – over six meters tall – in the world. The flightless grebes moved into this secret realm to perform their nest-building, egg-laying, and hatching of chicks. However, I could watch many pairs swim in and out with nest materials – rotting reed stalks, old cattail fronds, and fresh aquatic plants. Clearly they shared the task of nest-building. The first nest I managed to find measured a meter deep, nearly fifty centimeters in diameter, and must have weighed a hundred pounds! Only the top eight centimeters stood above the water's surface. It was anchored by two or three reed stalks. The underwater part was cone-shaped, providing stability in the winds and waves of Lake Atitlán. It was a well-built, impressive structure for two small birds. In my two years of field work at the lake, I discovered twenty grebe nests altogether. All were concealed inside thickets of reeds or cattails in more than a meter of water. But they were worth the trouble. Almost all contained eggs.

The first clutch I discovered held five eggs stained a mottled brown and about the size of hens' eggs. They lay in the nest's damp depression barely above lake level. The frightened female had deserted at my approach, covering her treasures with a blanket of pondweed, stonewort, old fronds, and the roots of water hyacinth. From the cover of dense reeds

**Game warden Edgar Bauer surveys reed beds from a patrol boat donated by the World Wildlife Fund**

**Juvenile grebe in Lake Atitlán. Since the bird's low point in the 1960s, numbers have jumped 300 per cent**

nearby, she uttered a low 'poc-poc-poc'. This is the call from which the Indians have derived their name for the grebes. Other nests I found never held more than five eggs. I calculated the average number at three – far less than the common pied-billed grebe's clutch size of from two to ten, with an average of six eggs.

Other differences between the common and giant species showed up during my field work. A few of the commons lived close by, yet they began nesting in January instead of April. Their young became independent much sooner than giant chicks. Common grebes fished and fed in the shallows close to shore, while the larger species sallied out from the reed beds and dived in much deeper waters. In short, I saw very little interaction between the two species and consider that each occupies a slightly different ecological niche.

Young giant grebes look like tiny black-and-white puffballs, with the lores and base of their bills bright salmon-orange. They are often transported on their parents' backs, huddled down among the scapular feathers between the wings. This helps to shield them from predatory fish, birds, or turtles. However, if the parent suddenly dives, the chicks may shake loose and pop to the surface.

These precocious little creatures cheep continuously unless warned by their parents. The thin penetrating lisp begins immediately after hatching and drying off, as does their ability to swim and dive. Watching intently through binoculars. I saw that this persistent begging

wins them a steady supply of water insects, crustaceans, and small fish, which are captured by both parents. Usually the female cares for half the brood, the male, the other half, during the ten to twelve weeks they are dependent. Unfortunately, chick survival is quite low. According to my studies, less than thirty-five per cent of the clutch hatch and reach the age of independence. After that, mortality is even higher. The main reason is that the bass have taken most of the aquatic food and what's left is often too large for the birds to cope with. For example, I once watched two parents present their fledgling with a small bass twenty-five times. The chick just could not swallow it, struggle as it might. Finally it gave up. I also hand-examined three juvenile grebes and found them so malnourished and emaciated that they probably died shortly thereafter. This was one of the unforeseen bad effects of the bass introduction.

Considering these problems, and the overall ecological imbalance of Lake Atitlán, I tried to find another Guatemalan lake where we might transfer the giant grebes for safer keeping. My search took me to practically every lake in that magnificent country. Yet none had the unique combination of factors that Atitlán had. Either they were too near human habitation, or too warm, or already stocked with bass, or did not offer safe habitat for the birds. Finally, it became obvious that only their natural home would serve, and we had better direct all our efforts to improving that area. Little could be done to control or eliminate the introduction of bass because the lake is so huge (ten cubic miles) that it would have taken ten trainloads of fish poison to wipe them out! Therefore, Operation Protection of the Poc doubled its efforts at law enforcement and conservation education. We also tried to improve other environmental factors and began to build a grebe sanctuary. My rationale was that if all else failed at Lake Atitlán, we could at least keep a small remnant population of giant grebes alive in the refuge.

I discussed the plan with the Division of Natural Resources in the Ministry of Agriculture. We decided to use a small bay called Xecamuc on the lake's south shore near Santiago Atitlán town and construct a visitor's center and sanctuary. Colonial Spanish priests had made a small fish hatchery here two to three centuries before. The low rock wall separating the bay from the main lake was in ruins, but we used it as a ready-made foundation. The wall was rebuilt with a four-meter mouth left at the center for freshwater exchange with the lake. Fencing was erected around the bay, over the wall, and across the mouth. This done, we treated the bay with fish toxicant to remove any big bass and restocked it with small native fishes donated by the Guatemalan Government.

On a small hill above the refuge, Indian stone masons labored to build a rustic, open-air, visitor's center with observatory, small office, a porch, sanitary facilities, and terraces. Inside, I hung a photographic display provided by the National Geographic Society and a primitive Indian *poc* painting. Tourists and birdwatchers can stop here to learn the story of the grebes, then travel out by boat to observe wild birds. During our construction of this refuge, I earned a nickname – 'Mama Poc'. The Indian laborers called me this because they marvelled that a *gringa* (Yankee girl) could show such concern over a few birds.

After many difficulties we managed to capture four birds and release them in the refuge. Then, finally, on 15 June 1968, the Ministry of Agriculture officially inaugurated this small sanctuary as its first national wildlife refuge. A year or two later, they built a dirt road into the area so that visitors may now arrive by boat *or* car. At this point, I relinquished my responsibilities to the Government and returned to Cornell University to finish my doctoral thesis about this project.

In 1969, the Guatemalan postal service issued a commemorative cover and three colorful airmail postage stamps featuring the giant grebes and Lake Atitlán. These were the most attractive stamps ever printed by this country and did much to spread the word about our conservation campaign. The cover reads: 'Let us Conserve the Grebe (*Podilymbus gigas*), or Poc.'

The crisis which confronted the Atitlán grebe has passed. The bird's trend towards extinction has been reversed, at least temporarily. Since 1968, I've managed to return almost every year to make a new census with the game warden at Lake Atitlán. Thus, we have documented the slow and steady increase of *pocs*. This spring (of 1977), we counted 233 birds. That means an increase of 300 per cent since the population's low point – which, we

Author Anne LaBastille holds a giant grebe in her hands after capturing it to put it into the grebe refuge, built to ensure that come what may at least some grebes survive

feel, shows that the conservation and management practices are proving beneficial.

At the same time, certain ecological adjustments have occurred. The bass and crappie populations have peaked and crashed and levelled off. The aquatic ecosystem has slowly readjusted to allow giant grebes, small fishes, crabs, insects, and bass to achieve a new, more stable balance. Lake Atitlán may never again hold its full complement of giant grebes and the fisheries will never be the same as before; however, now there are limited numbers of all these creatures. Perhaps the greatest benefit of the grebes' close brush with extinction has been to sound an alert for conservation in Guatemala. Just as the near-annihilation of egrets and herons in North America around 1900 made people aware of the urgent need to protect wild animals, so the plight of the *poc* made many Guatemalans conscious of their natural resources and their obligation to protect them.

In spite of the success of this conservation campaign, there are two disturbing developments lurking in the background. One is a $115 million hydroelectric plant for Lake Atitlán. Its construction has been contemplated since the early 1970s. To be financed by the World Bank and the Guatemalan National Institute for Electrification (INDE), the project calls for the huge basin of Lake Atitlán to be used as a natural reservoir. Underwater tunnels would draw off water and drop it 300 meters down through penstocks to turbines and generators on the Pacific slope. A power capacity of 500 megawatts is planned. This would drop lake levels forty feet or more over a ten-year span.

As partial replacement, four mountain rivers would be diverted into Lake Atitlán. Two of these are badly silted and polluted. Such diversions, it has been estimated by hydrologists, would totally change the clear aquamarine-blue waters to muddy-brown within seventy-seven years. The gem that is Lake Atitlán would no longer exist. Threatened would be the entire tourist trade, water recreation, source of drinking water, and aesthetic appeal of one of the most beautiful lakes in the world. In addition, since the disastrous earthquake of 1976, any tunnels and power lines running through this highly seismic zone would be far from safe.

The need for electricity in this developing country is unquestionable. Yet the methods and sources by which it is produced should be studied extremely carefully. The consequences of once again deranging Atitlán's aquatic ecosystem and environment, perhaps permanently, is too frightening. Many conservationists, including myself, have pointed this out to the Guatemalan Government by letters in the past three or four years. Twice the hydroelectric project has been set aside while alternatives are studied. At present, it is 'on the shelf', yet its shadow still lurks like a specter in the future.

The second problem is the craze of real estate development which is sweeping around Lake Atitlán. Shoreline property has skyrocketed in price and vacation homes and hotels are mushrooming. Many landowners are clearing shorelines of reeds and cattails to make beaches and docks. Grebe habitat is decreasing. Biggest of all is a three-tower, twelve-story condominium under construction on the north shore. I fear for the sewage disposal, the increase in boats on the lake, and the ultimate social impact on the simple Mayan Indians of the area.

We have already had a dramatic lesson on the dangers of exotic introductions into the environment and the need for solicitous stewardship of the ecological system. In the case of the bass introduction, natural biological forces and timely human ministrations gave the grebes a second chance. But the physical, chemical, and sociological changes resulting from a huge hydroelectric project and real estate development may prove too complex for repair.

As I gaze over the magnificent lake which harbors the world's only handful of giant grebes, plus its colorful local population of Mayan Indians, my fervent hope is that wise landuse planning and conservation education will save them and this priceless setting from destruction.

# ABBOTT'S BOOBY AND CONSERVATION

Bryan Nelson

Ten years ago, I was sitting up a *Eugenia* tree on the plateau of the Indian Ocean Christmas Island, fondly observing, at close range, one of the world's rarest and most beautiful seabirds. At that time, it was also one of the least known. It was not even collected and named until W. L. Abbott shot one on Assumption Island in September 1892 and as late as 1967 virtually nothing was known about its life history. Indeed, juvenile and immature birds had not knowingly been seen, as the inaccurate descriptions and illustrations, such as they were, made abundantly plain.

One can readily understand why a small, drab, burrowing petrel nesting high on inaccessible islands should remain obscure, but it might seem strange that a large, noisy booby, on an island inhabited by hundreds of Europeans and Australians, including a notable ornithologist (C. A. Gibson-Hill, of the Raffles Museum in Singapore), should maintain its mystery almost until the present decade. Yet it is not so strange, for the human activity on Christmas Island is highly specialized, and was until recently confined to a few small areas, leaving much more than ninety per cent of the island covered with jungle, largely untrodden. It took several days of continuous and often difficult walking for Gibson-Hill to cross the island on foot, even though it is nowhere more than about twelve miles long or wide. Whilst the other 199 'whites' were enjoying the fleshpots of their cosy little world in the settlement, Charles was making his solitary way through the jungle, pack on back. Moreover, his quarry was not nesting conveniently in colonies on the ground, but dispersed, high in the jungle canopy, usually totally obscured.

So Abbott's booby carried on as usual, hardly affected by the few tracks, the two small clearings from which the trees and soil had been removed to get at the rich deposits of calcium phosphate or, even, in the early 1940s, the occupation by Japanese forces. The mining concern was pleasantly and benevolently conducted in an old-fashioned British-colonial manner, the work force of Malays and Chinese was simple and happy, and hardly anybody in the world, including Australians, had ever heard of Christmas Island. Even if, by the end of World War II, they had, they still thought it was in the Pacific, and used as an atomic testing ground – as indeed was the case on the atoll of this name in the central Pacific Line Islands.

As in so many other cases, however, the 1960s on Christmas Island was a time of unprecedented 'development' and exploitation. Those years must surely mark the point at which the economists changed gear, and the old status of many delightful corners of the world changed alarmingly. For Christmas Island, they meant a momentous acceleration of effort in phosphate extraction, coinciding with the run-down of other sources, notably Ocean Island and Nauru. In 1958, Christmas Island, which had been annexed as an uninhabited island by Britain in 1888, became a Territory of the Commonwealth of Australia. Between times, it had been incorporated for administrative purposes with the Straits settlements, and Singapore law applied. This status was repealed in 1946 and from then until 1958 the island was governed and administered, along with the Cocos Keeling Islands, as a separate colony, known as the Colony of Singapore. Everything that has happened since 1958 has effectively been controlled by Australia, although New Zealand is equally involved in the actual mining of phosphate. The Phosphate Commission, still known for historical reasons as the British Phosphate Commission, is directed by Australian and New Zealand Commissioners. Until 1977, they exercised complete and virtually autonomous control over the island, so far as phosphate extraction is concerned. Indeed, until fairly recently they also ran virtually all other activities for the 3,000 Asians and 300 or so Europeans. These included education, medical care, transport, the post office, and radio. Now, however, the Australian Government is intimately involved and the island is controlled by the new, some-

**Female Abbott's booby. Though the world population may be 8,000 birds, they all breed on Christmas Island in the Indian Ocean, and because of the dense nature of the vegetation and the birds' habit of nesting high in the forest canopy, the species remained virtually unstudied until 1967**

70

what polyglot Department of Administration. These details are important in understanding the conservation issues.

In 1967, my wife and I landed on the island just in time to see it much as it had been for most of this century, and before the great leap forward. By sheer chance, subsequent events were destined to be much affected by this timing, for, with uncanny precision, we followed on the very heels of a rapidly-working team of surveyors and drillers, who were systematically covering the island on a grid basis. Hey presto! The wearisome, unproductive, and trackless journeys of Gibson-Hill were replaced by much easier and highly productive surveys by jeep and on foot along cleared tracks to all parts of the island. Without this, we could not have discovered the distribution and size of the population and there would have been no basis for estimating the effects, on Abbott's booby, of the projected plans for phosphate extraction, and none for conservation proposals.

At this point a brief summary of the conservation problem is appropriate. First and most important is the considerable overlap between the distribution of Abbott's booby and that of the best grade of phosphate. The booby inhabits mainly the central and western parts of the central plateau, above the 500-foot contour. The island consists of coralline limestone built on upraised volcanic rock and the central portion is bounded by an inland cliff which was at one time the sea-cliff. The geology is complex and hardly relevant here, but the factor common both to the occurrence of large phosphate deposits and the presence of Abbott's booby is irregular topography. This allows the accumulation of deposits and also provides emergent trees rather than a smooth canopy. Emergent trees are an important requirement of Abbott's booby.

The phosphate occurs in three grades – 'A', 'B', and 'C', defined by their percentages of nitrogen and phosphate. The boundaries of the 'fields' are not as precise as they look on the map, and there may well be areas of 'B' or 'C' within a field marked 'A'. This is not unimportant, as we shall see, but the main point is that 'A' fields are the most valuable and are those which overlap with Abbott's distribution. The deposits of 'B' grade are vastly larger, and of 'C' grade almost unlimited – there being little difference between 'C' grade and the

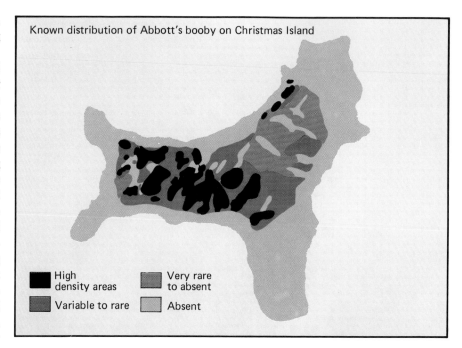

Known distribution of Abbott's booby on Christmas Island

High density areas
Variable to rare
Very rare to absent
Absent

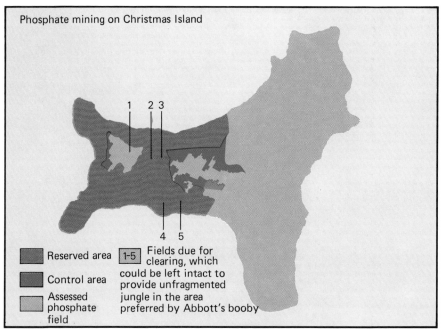

Phosphate mining on Christmas Island

1 2 3
4 5

Reserved area
Control area
Assessed phosphate field
1-5 Fields due for clearing, which could be left intact to provide unfragmented jungle in the area preferred by Abbott's booby

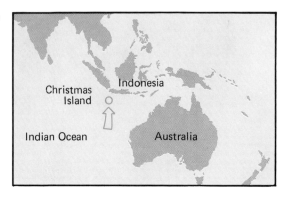

Christmas Island
Indonesia
Indian Ocean
Australia

During mining operations on Christmas Island, the British Phosphate Commissioners have left 'tree islands' (top right) where any boobies have shown signs of nesting. This has undoubtedly saved many birds. Re-afforestation is another key element of the conservation effort (bottom right) but will take at least fifty years general overburden or top-covering of the whole island. 'B' and 'C' grades tend to occur on the lower terraces, which are in many places quite unworkable because of the massive limestone pinnacles which would have to be removed. It is thus quite true that the projected extraction of 'A' grade would still leave large areas of Christmas Island under jungle, even if most of it would be useless for Abbott's booby. The problems are therefore simply stated, if nonetheless intractable: how much of Abbott's preferred habitat will remain when all the grade 'A' fields have been cleared? Will this be adequate for the species' needs (remembering that there are no other known breeding places in the world)? Can it be made inhabitable again in time?

These problems invite consideration of the other main 'difficulty', with which they mesh. This is the exceptionally slow reproductive rate of Abbott's booby. Not only does it lay but a single egg; it does so only once in two years. Moreover, an extraordinarily high proportion (almost certainly more than ninety per cent) of its young die before they reach independence. There may be occasional years in which the success rate is higher, but the three breeding cycles for which we have evidence have all been extremely unsuccessful.

The corollary is that the adults must be extraordinarily longlived simply in order to replace themselves. This means that they are highly non-expendable. The population is extremely vulnerable to any reduction in numbers, or in recruitment rate, and has almost no elasticity. It is plodding away on very long-term contracts with its selection-pressures, perhaps fluctuating in numbers over long periods of time (we don't know), but certainly incapable of calling on short-term increases in recruitment to offset any reduction in the population. If loss of habitat were to result in even lower recruitment in Abbott's booby, either through the birds attempting to use sub-optimal nesting trees and failing more often, or simply by reducing the number that attempt to breed, then a long-term slide, which would be extremely difficult to detect until far advanced, could be set in motion. The possible reasons for the evolution of the unusual reproductive cycle and low success of Abbott's booby are fascinating, but, to complete the conservation aspects first, let me briefly summarize events since 1967.

Up to and including 1971, implementing the decision to increase output, the British Phosphate Commissioners cleared several mid-plateau areas, including, in Fields 19, 20, 21, and 22, some of the forest most densely inhabited by Abbott's booby. This displaced a substantial number of pairs and destroyed some, possibly many, adults and young birds. At that time the conservation issue was not thought to be important, or even to exist. Abbott's booby was still hardly known. The publication in 1971, of the 1967 study, generated rather more awareness and the International Council for Bird Preservation (ICBP), among others, became concerned. Events culminated in Australia, in 1974, in a House of Representatives Standing Committee Report on Christmas Island and Conservation, to which I gave evidence, and the XVIth International Ornithological Congress and the 1974 World Conference of the ICBP, both of which were held in the same month in Canberra. Australia was very much in the center of the world ornithological stage, and was becoming fully aware that, in Christmas Island among other places, she had a notable jewel. It should be recalled that, besides Abbott's, Christmas Island possesses several other endemic species, including Andrew's frigate, the beautiful golden bosun bird, a goshawk, the Christmas Island imperial pigeon, and a delightful little owl, together with a rare and beautiful forest complex, in some ways unique, and a wonderful invertebrate fauna. Perhaps of relevance, also, was the 1974 production of a film I made in 1967, showing Abbott's booby, for the first time, in the next best medium to flesh and blood. It is easier to get excited about a lovely and impressive bird than about mere figures. There were two more helpful events. Most important and fortunate, was the presence on the island throughout this critical period of a BPC surveyor and splendid naturalist, David Powell, who was deeply concerned about Abbott's booby. The other was the opportunity, which I was offered in 1974, of re-visiting the island and assessing the impact of the changes that had occurred since 1967.

The upshot of this unusual concentration of attention was twofold. First, the 1974 Standing Committee made some important conservation proposals, including the setting aside of the densest Abbott's areas regardless of the phosphate. Second, the Phosphate Com-

As part of the effort to rehabilitate the areas of the island which have been mined for phosphate, surveyor and naturalist David Powell has established a flourishing nursery (above) of the key emergent trees favored by Abbott's booby. Many juvenile boobies fall on their first flight, but since the species' rate of reproduction is so slow, David Powell helps maintain numbers by persuading these grounded youngsters to return to their nests (right)

missioners, voluntarily and out of genuine concern, appointed David Powell as full-time conservator in 1974.

The conservation proposals never became law, because the Whitlam government fell. However, they were followed in 1975 by a visit to the island of an Environmental Reconnaissance Team who later presented a comprehensive management plan for the conservation of the island, including, of course, the booby. Meantime, David Powell had been busy, independently implementing a program of 'selective clearing', to which the Reconnaissance Team eventually gave their backing. Their report states the policy of the present Australian Government. Over-simplifying, it has three main strands: selective clearing under controlled conditions; the setting aside of an inviolable reserve area; and the rehabilitation of despoiled areas.

Selective clearing means that all trees which hold a nest, a pair, or even a single 'interested' Abbott's booby, in areas being cleared of forest, are left standing until the breeding attempt is over. Obviously it entails a great deal of hard work on the part of the conservator, and inconvenience for BPC, but it has undoubtedly saved many boobies from destruction. Since the adults are so long-lived, this is enormously worthwhile. But eventually the jungle is cleared. The Commissioners deserve great credit for voluntarily adopting this policy; more than one big mining company behaves much less responsibly. The only question concerns the longer-term effect of destruction of the birds' preferred nesting areas. Here the Reconnaissance Team report is clearly weaker than were the earlier Standing Committee's recommendations. The former proposes to continue selective clearing subject to 'control', which means consultation with the resident Government Conservator (not David Powell, who continues as the BPC Conservator). The Government Conservator is responsible for ensuring that jungle clearings proposed by the BPC are compatible with conservation needs, but reasonably enough, his department is also concerned to ensure that phosphate extraction meets its commitments. So, instead of giving any crucial phosphate areas 'full reserve" status, it is hoped to proceed as hitherto, keeping a watchful eye on Abbott's, and ready to stop clearing anywhere, if it seems necessary. The snag is that it is virtually impossible to say if and when it *is* necessary! In fact, however, most of the controversial clearing has already been completed, although isolated stands of forest have been left here and there, where the presence of Abbott's boobies forbade clearing. These 'islands' are extensively used by the boobies even amidst the general devastation of the area, with cranes and Euclid trucks thundering around beneath them.

Since at least 1974, the BPC have curbed the enthusiasm, natural to the genre, of their engineers, and restricted clearance to essentials, where before they simply flattened everything (it is so much tidier, on the drawing board, to start operations in a vast, clean rectangle rather than a messy, cluttered polygon). This care will continue. In 1977 they were just completing extensive clearances in the Murray Hill segment, their last big area of top-grade phosphate. With the burgeoning and now truly massive costs of extraction and administration, they could hardly continue at all without it.

Murray Hill is thick with Abbott's. In January 1977 Dave Powell and I had eleven nests under observation in a few trees left standing amidst the forest wreckage of what will soon be No. 4 loading bay complete with railroad head! Goshawks skulked, imperial pigeons cooed, Abbott's shouted, and white-eyes hunted, titmouse-like, where shortly will be steel, concrete, and huge heaps of phosphate. So Murray Hill has partly gone. However, one of the most valuable recommendations of the Reconnaissance Team is that part of the remaining Murray Hill area be given full Reserve Status. If to that could be added five more small areas (see map) there would be a respectable block of *unfragmented* forest in the center and south-west of the island, which is the preferred habitat of Abbott's booby. This, with the continuing preservation of the adult stock, seems to me the best balance that can be achieved between the conflicting interests of conservation and phosphate mining. If, at some future date, long-term research shows that Abbott's booby is breeding as successfully on the fringes of its destroyed areas and in the 'tree islands', as it is in pristine habitat, and if re-afforestation is going well, these reserved phosphate areas will still be there for exploitation.

To this, one might ask, 'what will the Phosphate Commissioners actually do?'. Pre-sent times are complex and difficult for them. They are now, for the first time, faced with union activity on the island and there is the not-too-distant probability that the rules under which Asian labor is permitted entry to Christmas Island will be changed. The whole atmosphere has changed for the worse, and rocketing labor costs could pose crucial economic problems for the future viability of phosphate extraction. This could be a good or a disastrous thing for conservation. If it curtails future mining activities, conservation will benefit. But if it produces pressure for massively up-scaled and highly mechanized extractions including that of the low grade deposits, then greatly increased clearance will follow.

On a more biological note, there are several points which I raised and deferred in passing, and which underlie the whole strategy of conservation of Abbott's booby. These are: population size and the nature of the breeding cycle; the use of sub-optimal habitat; the possibility of rehabilitation; and (though I did not raise it) the idea of transferring Abbott's elsewhere.

The world population is probably around 8,000 free-flying individuals, including dependent juveniles and immature birds. This figure, higher than my upper estimate (5,500) of 1967, is based on more exhaustive counts of inflying birds by David Powell. Of these, probably no more than 700 pairs lay in any one year, which puts the size and value of the breeding population in true perspective. The egg is laid between May and July and the chick grows so slowly that by the time the weather breaks for the 'winter', often with strong winds, low cloud, and heavy rain between November and March, it is nowhere near fledging let alone independence. Consequently, it has to sit it out in the tree-tops until things improve again the next year. But those three or four bad months are usually more than it can survive on the generally irregular and widely spaced feeds which are all that it gets. Only a fraction of the prospering August chicks live through it. Many fall, or fail their first flight in January or February. David Powell has established a rookery of grounded juveniles in his garden, but it is a long job – often more than six months – before they become independent. Others are successfully returned to their tree-top nests. Normally a young Abbott's booby can expect to be fed for much more than a

**An adult booby with chick. The young develop very slowly, and are not ready to leave the nest before the weather breaks for the 'winter'. Only a fraction of each year's chicks survive, and they can expect to be fed for much more than a year after hatching**

year after hatching. Clearly, with such a low recruitment rate, population trends, and hence conservation measures, cannot be judged in less than decades.

The preference of Abbott's booby for certain areas of the island lies at the root of the conservation problem. The birds have demonstrated the strength of this attachment beyond doubt both by remaining in trees, even single ones, left standing in cleared areas, and by moving only to the very fringes of such areas in preference to moving right away to undisturbed forest. Clearly, a key question for future research is the relative success of such birds. Until we know much more, the preservation of a large block of unfragmented jungle in or around the original preferred habitat is essential.

Re-afforestation is another Powell baby. He has established a flourishing nursery of the key emergent jungle trees favored by Abbott's. Furthermore, for the future, the Reconnaissance Team recommend an integrated program of extraction and automatic back-filling, so that the daunting wastes of naked limestone pinnacles will not recur. There are practical snags, principally the reluctance of the BPC, for good practical reasons, to mine an area so completely that they can then unequivocally abandon it. However, total mining is future policy. But re-afforestation will take at least fifty years and possibly considerably longer. Whilst eminently desirable, it is not a solution

in itself. Finally, it seems quite impracticable to transfer Abbott's booby anywhere else. First, one would have to find a suitably forested island in the right region (Abbott's probably feeds in an area of ocean upwelling off Java), though there is no overriding reason why the Chagos Archipelago would not be suitable. Second, one would have to hand-raise young birds actually on the target island, enough of them to withstand the inevitable mortality during transition to independence and still leave a reasonable number to establish nesting pairs. This would mean rearing about a hundred young for almost a year. Then, one would have to assume that the liberated boobies would like the island enough to return, even though they had been born on Christmas Island. Transferred adults would of course simply return to Christmas Island.

So the best solution clearly is to leave enough of Christmas Island to support the existing population of Abbott's booby. It may well be that the present population is extremely finely balanced, with recruitment just enough to replace the losses due to the harsh demands of its unusual life cycle. I doubt if there are any density-dependent factors limiting the size of the population: it simply cannot produce more young in the face of the severe limitations imposed by the winters, and the biennial breeding. If this is so, the number of Abbott's boobies in existence neither aids nor hinders the survival of individuals, since there is no competitition for any essential resource. But, and here is the rub, the actual number may be critical when the population has to absorb a long run of above-average breeding failures. It cannot call on reserve mechanisms to boost the birth-rate, and if total numbers fall, their restitution may be impossible. Then the population would be at the mercy of external factors. A long run of good years could resuscitate it; a run of bad years could take it below the threshold for recovery.

On balance, the prospects are much more hopeful than seemed probable a decade ago, and the establishment of a sufficiently large reserve forest area, along with selective clearing, reafforestation, and careful research and monitoring of the population, should be enough to save Abbott's – to the very real credit of Australia and the British Phosphate Commissioners.

# OTHER ANIMALS

## PROTECTING INDIA'S SNAKES

Romulus and Zahida Whitaker

Government legislation protecting snakes came to India not a minute too early. In the past, millions of snakes were killed every year to supply the skin trade, regardless of the species, its status, or the breeding season. Statistics for 1968, for example, indicate that no less than 10,000,000 snakes (valued at over Rs 107 million) were slaughtered. Rare species such as pythons, flying snakes, and king cobras ended up in the over-crowded morass of the live reptile trade. Inevitably, up to eighty per cent perished before reaching their destination. In 1968 a recorded ninety-three live pythons and twenty-seven live king cobras were sold through the Calcutta market alone.

As in the frog-leg industry, the skinning of snakes was done in a manner to assure maximum profits and minimum overheads; consequently cobras, pythons, and other snakes were often skinned alive and left to die. which, to judge by the tenacity of reptiles, could take days. In rural areas near Madras it is still not unusual to find the carcasses of skinned snakes lying near dug-out rat burrows. During the egg-laying season a female rat snake or cobra, heavy with eggs, is most vulnerable and is not spared.

The skin market catered mostly to the western European countries and more recently to the newly 'luxury'-minded nations such as Yugoslavia, Czechoslavakia, and the Soviet Union. The industry boomed in the late 1950s and 1960s and tanning centers were busy activating catchers (tribal peoples) all over India. The proprietor of one of the best known tanneries in Madras regularly handled up to 10,000 skins a day during the peak years.

The 1975–6 Export Policy for Wildlife Products put a brake on this uncontrolled harvest. Under this law, export of live snakes or their products, including venom and skins, is normally not allowed. The ban is lifted from time to time, probably according to pressure from skin business magnates. In 1976 the World Wildlife Fund office in Calcutta reported the export of two and a half tons of snake skins; it turned out that the Commerce Ministry had relaxed the ban to allow clearance of old stocks. This is a convenient opening for dealers; quickly accumulated fresh skins are easily passed off as 'old stock'. Working as we do at the Madras Snake Park with the Irula tribal snake catchers, news about the underworld skin market reaches us fairly quickly!

The other protective legislation which covers Indian snakes is the Wildlife (Protection) Act of 1972 which encompasses all Indian animal life and provides stringent protection for endangered and rare species. The only snakes included in the act are the pythons (the Indian rock python, found throughout India, and the reticulated python, found only in the Nicobar Islands). These are listed under Schedule II, which means that pythons can in fact be hunted under conditions specified in a special license issued by the State Chief Wildlife Warden. The license holder must maintain a record of animals killed or captured during the currency of the license, and submit this to the state warden.

Although no other snake is protected by the

**The reticulated python, found in the Nicobar Islands in India, is one of only two snakes (the other is the rock python) protected by the Indian Wildlife (Protection) Act of 1972**

Act, rules have been framed for trade, possession, and capture of wild animals, and this includes all species of snakes. A snake catcher must have a capture license and a dealer needs purchase, possession, sale, and transport permits. Again, both seller and buyer must submit records to the Forest Department officials.

Implementation of these complicated laws in a country like ours where few tribals can read or write is not an easy matter. However, the wildlife authorities are on the whole active and interested and in many parts of the country have carried out surprise raids on unlicensed dealers. The job of preventing illegal trade in skins is monumental: it is a well established and very profitable business and the number of dealers involved is too great for the small band of authorized officials to cope with. Customs authorities could play an important role in clamping down on the sale and smuggling of unlicensed snake skins.

Skin markets are still regular features in several towns of South India, and the majority of these deal in unlicensed skins. While on a tour of Pudukkottai District in January 1975 we stumbled on a Friday skin bazaar and photographed meter-high mounds of skins, most of them from cobras, rat snakes, and Russell's vipers. We were shown dozens of fresh salted python skins awaiting purchase.

The rat snake has been the basis of the long uncontrolled skin industry since its beginning in the 1930s. Indications are that rat infestation is a growing problem in areas that have been major skin centers. In fact, many farmers realize the significance of this and we have been several times chased away by conservation-minded farmers while snake-hunting with Irula tribals! Tea estates and orchards in the southern hills, where felling and burning have eliminated predators such as snakes and owls, complain of substantial losses each year from destruction of tea bushes and grain by rats. One such sufferer even requested that the Madras Snake Park release a load of rat snakes in the area!

Although no quantitative work has so far been done on the rodent controlling capacity of snakes, there is no doubt that snakes are indispensable predators. The number of adult rats taken per week by a captive rat snake varies from three to six; in the wild the number may be more, and would include entire broods of young. Although birds of prey are effective rodent eaters, snakes are the only Indian animals that have the ability to actually follow and kill rats down inside the hole. In fact, the sand boas with their blunt shovel-shaped heads and burrowing habits are the only effective controls for the prolific and destructive mole rat. Millions of rupees are spent annually on deadly poisons which are poured into the ground in an effort to reduce rat populations. While this dangerous operation goes on minimal attention is paid to natural biocontrol – the constant free service of snakes in our agro-ecology. Studies of rodent control in the wild by snakes would produce some very interesting results. These could perhaps be undertaken jointly with the Irula tribals, who are masters of the natural history of snakes and rats (snakes are hunted for skins and venom, and rats for meat and stored grain).

Several little-known species of snakes suffer from factors other than killing for the skin trade, such as loss of habitat. One such snake is the king cobra, the most magnificent and intelligent of all snakes, which lives mainly in the hills of southern and northern India at altitudes of 500 to 1,500 meters. Most of the range is now under tea and coffee and in these plantation areas king cobras are shot or beaten to death whenever seen. As larger areas are cleared and brought under cultivation they are left with less and less optimum habitat.

Shieldtails or uropeltids, a unique group of beautifully iridescent burrowing snakes, live in the cool tropical forest areas of the hills. They are rapidly losing habitat as rain forests are clear-felled for timber and agriculture or cut down to make way for dams and hydroelectric projects. The felling of the large trees brings about drastic changes in forest floor temperatures, eliminating many species of snakes, frogs, and lizards. As India insists on travelling the fateful road to 'development' many species are losing irretrievable ground. The change of environment coupled with the heavy hands of men employed to change it, promises long-term damage. During a visit to the Agumbe rain forest in 1976, our ears were assailed with the groans and crashing of falling trees; scattered around the felling camp were carcasses of the beautiful hump-nosed pit viper.

The preservation of these and other rare and interesting snakes is possible only by retaining

**Pit vipers (right) are amongst a long list of Indian snakes that are suffering from the continuing felling of rain forest to make way for agriculture, dams, and hydroelectric projects. Ignorance and fear are responsible for the demise of many snakes in India. The sand boa (bottom right) is wrongly supposed to spread leprosy. In fact, it is really a very useful animal and is the only effective control for the prolific and destructive mole rat**

**(Over page) One of the four common dangerous snakes in India, the cobra is slaughtered in large numbers for the skin trade. Yet it is a species that may survive longer than most, as it is highly adaptable and thrives on the increase in rodents resulting from expanding agriculture**

the tropical forest areas, which are usually of vital importance as watersheds and reservoirs of forest resources. While cobras, rat snakes, and other open-land species are highly adaptable to changes in environment (thriving, in fact, on the increase in rodents brought about by increased agriculture), forest species such as pythons, king cobras, pit vipers, and uropeltids need their very specialized habitats. With their specific temperature, humidity, elevational, and vegetation preferences they could be used to monitor the environmental quality of forests in the country.

Ignorance and fear are the other enemies of snake conservation. Almost every snake is believed to be venomous and is killed on sight. Then it is burned with the proper rites and ceremonies to prevent 'revenge' by the snake's mate. It is wrongly believed that the harmless vine snake blinds people by striking at the eyes; that the common sand boa spreads leprosy; that the (venomous) krait can suck the breath away from a man as he sleeps. The stories are endless; the fear that causes them is understandable. Millions of Indians live in villages beyond reach of the life-saving antivenin serum, and snakebite is looked on with fatalism and fear. While living in villages we have been called many times to help snakebite victims. Transport was often non-existent and time was frequently wasted trying out village 'remedies' in the form of charms and herbal treatments. Most times, the patient would be dead by the time we got there with antivenin. Most nocturnal bites were by kraits; the symptoms are delayed and then dramatic, sometimes appearing suddenly, several hours after the bite. This occasional 'stroke of doom' helps to perpetuate the superstitious dread of all snakes.

At the Madras Snake Park we stress in every demonstration, lecture, and display that there are four common dangerous snakes in India – the cobra, krait, Russell's viper, and saw-scaled viper, and once these can be easily identified there is no cause for fear of snakes in general. Easier said than done! Cobras resemble rat snakes, kraits resemble harmless wolf snakes, saw-scaled vipers resemble cat snakes and Russell's vipers look like the common sand boa. Besides, the one million visitors we have at the Snake Park each year speak some fourteen different languages, and have a wealth of inherited snake folk-lore within them.

However, from the increasing numbers of visitors, enquiries, and appeals for information, it is evident that some beginning has been made.

During demonstrations and lectures the subject of snakebites is also touched upon and people are told, repeatedly, that antivenin serum is the only cure. The seminar on snakebite held in August 1977, convened by the Madras Snake Park and the Madras Medical College, was a major breakthrough and methods of educating the masses about the use of antivenin and getting it to them were formulated. Once fear, and with it the unpleasant stigma attached to snakes, is removed through education, conservation of these reptiles will be far easier. Snake parks are a good medium for this kind of wildlife education; the main difficulty is finding interested individuals to take on the responsibility of caring properly for large numbers of live snakes.

Although serpents feature prominently in Hindu mythology and religion, this unfortunately does not aid the living snake in the manner that the cow is benefitted by its mythological past. (Among some sects of Hindus, however, killing a snake is considered to be a sin, and snakes living in one's compound are thought to be a lucky sign.)

Wildlife conservation is complex at many levels; its effect on the 'ecosystem people' is typified by the plight of tribal snake-catching groups such as the Irulas in the new world of wildlife regulations and restrictions. Both in the past and today, the skin trade allows very little profit to the tribals. These are the people who have been the backbone of the industry – and their knowledge of the natural history of snakes need not die out. Based on studies to determine an ecologically sound sustained yield that could be obtained from snake skins, an industry should be set up exclusively for Irula tribals: a Wildlife Cooperative to be run by and for tribals. While the cooperative would have advisors to maintain checks on breeding seasons and quantity control, the project should be managed so as to ensure maximum profits for the Irulas, by eliminating the middle man.

A proposal outlining a venom and skin industry has been presented to the government and is under consideration. Numerous tribal groups besides the Irulas – such as the Gonds, Mahrs, and Muthurasa – have been victims of

**Although the Indian python is protected by law, it may still be hunted under a special license**

the wildlife legislation introduced recently. Although this is to an extent inevitable, it is tragic to see these hunter-gatherer groups turn to city jobs and slums, losing both their culture and knowledge of natural history. There are over 100,000 Irulas in Tamil Nadu state and nearly one-third have been involved in the snake skin and venom industry. A cooperative would ensure their future as well as the no-waste project that alone can justify wildlife exploitation.

People argue that the entire industry should be wiped out once and for all. This could perhaps be valid for the affluent nations; but in India conservation can 'work' only when geared toward considering wildlife a valuable natural resource which could pay its own way. If no direct economic value is placed on wildlife there will be no wild land set aside to harbor it. Lands and forests are in great demand and will not be preserved, it seems, for what may be called the 'luxury' of conservation or preservation.

Controlled exploitation by a cooperative would involve a small percentage of the numbers taken by the present-day skin trade, pet industry, biosupply trade, and incidental killing of snakes. Scientific researchers also take a toll of snake numbers: a study project in the Pacific sponsored by an American university collected nearly 15,000 sea snakes in summer field trips made in 1967, 1969, and 1972.

Studies on and publicity for snakes as rodent destroyers would help to create a more tolerant atmosphere for snakes, as would increased distribution of antivenin serum. Negative fear can be transformed to positive interest, when the 'terrible, slimy snake' is presented as a clean, dry, colorful, fascinating, and useful member of our world.

Banded krait (above) in the 'head under' defensive posture. Though poisonous, the krait suffers unduly from the myth that it can suck the breath away from a man as he sleeps. A beautiful green whip snake (top right) and the rare and little known king cobra (bottom right). The latter lives in areas which are largely being planted with tea and coffee, and the estate workers beat the snakes to death or shoot them on sight

# SAVING THE WOOD ANT

David Black

International Project 1380 of the World Wildlife Fund is unusual in that it features an invertebrate animal, the ant. Although much has been written about ants, about their behavior and social structure, the idea of ants being of direct benefit to man is a relatively new concept. Scientific studies of wood ants have been led for the past decade by the Germans – and in particular Professor Carl Gosswald, who has disseminated information throughout Europe from his small headquarters in the town of Wurzburg in southern Germany. The practicalities of wood ant conservation have now appeared in the leading biological journals and have become part of the practice of forest management in Switzerland, Italy, Holland, and Rumania, as well as in Germany itself.

The subjects of Professor Gosswald's work are the wood ants, especially *Formica rufa* and its close relative *Formica polyctena*. Although different in social structure and organization, both species are essential components of a healthy forest. People living and working in the forests have noticed green 'islands' of trees where ants' nests are present – in areas where the trees were otherwise denuded of pine needles and leaves by insects pests. This phenomenon was first recorded in the eighteenth century.

Gosswald was convinced that it was the ants which were responsible for these healthy islands of green in otherwise sterile tracts of forest. He was right, and the statistics involved are astounding. It has been calculated that a healthy colony of wood ants takes, on average, some 100,000 insects every day during the summer months; many of these are the larvae and adults of moths and sawflies that feed on oak, spruce, pine, and larch – all economically important trees.

Worker ants are constantly on the move, streaming out to cover a circular area of from twenty-five to 100 meters from the main nest, and extending upwards as a cylinder to the topmost branches of the trees. This territory is constantly scoured for prey, day and night. Flying insects that are too swift for the ants to catch during the day fall easy prey as they rest on the branches of trees and bushes at night.

The vicinity of an ants' nest is clearly not the best site for a laboratory for entomologists interested in the life cycle of the sawfly, for instance. Other biologists claim that the forest birdlife is impoverished because of ants: but this does not hold true, because ants in their search for prey are constantly dislodging large insects which are readily snapped up by tits and warblers and other small birds. The prime role of ants, and the most obvious, is therefore the destruction of insect pests, particularly the defoliators of the forest trees. Their other roles are less obvious and it is helpful to take a close look at a typical nest and its occupants in order to discover more about their interactions with the outside world.

A typical nest of *Formica rufa* is one meter high and several meters in circumference. The nest is usually developed around an old tree stump and has galleries deep into the soil; it is normally located in a forest glade or clearing where it receives the maximum amount of sunlight. A typical colony of *F. rufa* may have 150 to 200 queens and 6,000 workers, while the smaller *Formica polyctena* ants, which make smaller visible mounds, may have as many as a million workers and up to 5,000 queens. Impressive though these figures are, colonies of the latter species have a tendency to amalgamate into super-colonies where over fifty main nests and thirty secondary ones are interconnected by some eight kilometers of underground galleries.

Wood ants are mainly carnivorous, and have a very varied diet. Their main weapon in attack and defense is a concentrated solution of formic acid which is shot out in a jet from the mouth to immobilize prey and deter enemies. But for all this they nevertheless have a more lovable side: they are passionately fond of the wood aphids' honeydew and will go to great lengths to protect them. (These aphids

**Wood ants are an essential component of a healthy forest, and as long ago as the eighteenth century the association was noted between healthy green islands of trees and the presence of ants' nests**

are not harmful to trees. They suck the sap, or more correctly pierce the tree and suck the manufactured food substances in solution from the wood, rather than inject poisonous saliva into the tree, as is the common practice among garden aphids, which also attack the plant intra-cellularly.)

The ants lap up the honeydew exuding from the aphids' abdomens. They stroke and pamper them, move them on to fresher pastures, and in particular protect them by killing their predators. By maintaining a healthy aphid population, wood ants maintain healthy populations of bees – which also thrive on the aphids' sweet excretions. For this reason people who rear bees and keep hives in and around the forests are eager to protect and encourage wood ants in their area. Wood ants are also partial to the microscopic 'blooms' of fungi that form on the outer coverings of seeds. On finding a seed, an ant will carry it away, eat the outer covering, then dump it, often several meters from the parent plant. If one multiplies this activity 100,000 times one can see the immense value of the wood ant as a dispersal agent of woodland plants. In a similar way the activities of thousands of ants going to and from the nest enrich the forest soil with a constant supply of humus and other organic material.

Though the nest may seem secure enough, it is in fact vulnerable, and the ant has many enemies. The beetle *Clythra* is arch-enemy number one: the female beetle lets her eggs covered with debris fall on to the nest; on hatching, the beetle larvae enter the nest and gorge themselves on the plentiful supply of ant eggs, larvae, and pupae. The small wasp *Elasmosoma* attacks worker ants: the egg is deftly placed on the worker's body; when the egg hatches, the larva eats its way through the ant's abdomen. More conspicuous predators are woodpeckers, particularly the green woodpecker which is capable of digging into the very heart of the nest, especially in winter when the ants are torpid. Foxes and badgers also dig up ants' nests, though they are not after ants but the fat grubs of the beetle *Cetonia* which live in the mold of ant heaps. Last but not least comes man – whose various activities have caused a marked decrease in red ant populations, especially in the last decade.

An ants' nest arouses our curiosity, and many people see it as a challenge. Unfortunately, too many of us immediately want to kick at it or open it up with a stick. This, however, disturbs the delicate micro-climate of the anthill. The workers quickly swarm about the disturbance to repair the damage, but too often whole anthills are mutilated and razed to the ground. The ant colony is destroyed. Such destruction can be commonly seen around picnic spots in German and Swiss forests; in these places few anthills are allowed to remain intact. While adults have a rest, their children are out 'ant-bashing'.

The increased use of insecticides is another factor in the decline of the wood ant. They tend to favor land at the edges of woods and forests, in zones between two habitats where biological productivity is at its greatest, but they suffer as their insect prey is contaminated by chemicals sprayed on adjacent fields. Forest workers are often inclined to ignore, or even destroy, ants' nests when felling trees. Here the cause is a mixture of curiosity and ignorance – coupled with an innate wish to destroy. Wood ants are protected in both Germany and Switzerland, but wildlife laws don't always mean a great deal, even in these educated countries.

It is because of the decline in wood ant populations, and their immense value to man, that Gosswald and his colleagues have for some years carried out an extraordinary and far-sighted conservation campaign. Two practical measures involve the physical protection of the nest, and the artificial rearing and re-establishment of new colonies throughout the forests. To protect the nest a guard has been devised in the shape of a cupola or pyramid, comprising a frame of wood or metal surrounded by strong, wide-meshed netting. The guard is securely placed over the nest and inspected regularly. Several thousands of these guards have now been installed in Germany and Switzerland. The World Wildlife Fund has encouraged young people to help, and it has become something of a trend for youngsters to get involved with the building and placement of these guards in the forests. At least thirty-five forest districts in Germany use these protective measures.

The second main method of ant conservation involves taking ants and vegetable matter from a main nest and establishing a new colony in an area where the wood ant has declined. Collection of the ants takes place in the spring.

One conservation measure is placing a cupola-shaped guard over an ant-hill to provide protection. With World Wildlife Fund encouragement, young people in Germany and Switzerland have been carrying out the building and placement of these guards. There are now several thousand of them in German and Swiss forests

At this time, when the sun starts to warm the nest, the ants gradually move upwards from their winter quarters. It is also during spring that the queens are found near the surface. A successful scoop from an ants' nest must contain about 150 to 200 liters of material – pine needles, eggs, pupae, worker ants, and at least a hundred queens. The ant material is then placed in a special container and carried to a selected spot where a heap of brushwood and loose earth encourages the ants to found a new colony. A healthy forest should have one ants' nest for every two to three hectares (five to seven acres) of forest.

Another conservation method is to strengthen new colonies by taking advantage of the enormous surplus of queens produced each year; many of these are not readily accepted in the nest and easily fall victim to predators. The method Gosswald has used is to cover the nest in spring with a cone of dark cloth with an opening at the top. The young ants are attracted to the light, come to the surface, and are caught in a transparent receptacle such as a glass tank. Some nests produce nearly all females, others an abundance of males. The males and females can be encouraged to mate by lining the receptacle with moist earth and bark and keeping it partly in direct sunlight. To enrich a small existing colony with the newly mated queens it is necessary to first give them the 'colony odor' by introducing the queens to a few hundred workers from the nest which is to be added to. The potential of artificial rearing, although realized only recently, is well under way in several forest centers.

The World Wildlife Fund project involves a whole range of activities starting with surveys of numbers and species of wood ants. Training courses have been set up for teachers and foresters. The nest guards are constructed, and above all a general educational program has been mounted through the press and other media to inform the public about the value of the wood ant.

Many conservation projects are concerned with the larger (and, to some people, more glamorous) mammals and birds. But smaller animals are often just as important in the scheme of things. The wood ant is of direct material benefit to man, and its conservation is therefore very important to us. This is what the educational program will be trying to get across, and it is to be hoped that a change in man's traditional attitude towards ants will be the result.

**The number of ants can be increased by taking ants and vegetable matter from the main nest and establishing a new colony elsewhere in the forest (left). The material collected (here being carefully poured on the ground) contains pine needles, eggs, pupae, worker ants, and at least a hundred queens.**
**An alternative to the cupola-shaped guards, the guard on the right also serves to protect the ants from their natural enemies, particularly the woodpeckers which like to feed on them in winter**

# BOG BUTTERFLIES OF SOUTHERN FINLAND

Leigh Plester

Around ten thousand years ago Europe's most recent glaciation came to an end. As the ice retreated through northern Europe it was followed by a belt of coniferous forest, or taiga. The creeping glaciers had dragged with them large boulders which gouged hollows in the bedrock and as the ice melted many of these filled with water to become today's typically shallow Fennoscandian lakes. Others became dominated by sphagnum and similar mosses with a remarkable capacity for retaining water and thus forming bogs.

The acidity of such bogs is often so acute that only certain specialized higher plants can come to terms with it. Sphagnum bogs are encroached upon by such plants, which include pine, bog rosemary, bog whortleberry, cotton grass and sedges, cranberry, crowberry, marsh andromeda, and cloudberry. Upon reaching a certain height – usually three or four meters – the trees (mainly pine) wither and die, and their gnarled and stunted pale gray skeletons dotted about a bog seem as timeless and supernatural as the Aku-Aku monuments.

Dead plant material inevitably collapses on to the bog surface, into which it gradually sinks. It does not decay because the acidic conditions deter the bacteria normally active at sylvan sites of death and decay. Finally, enough debris accumulates to provide other kinds of trees with a strong, drier foundation. More water is absorbed than is provided by annual precipitation. Under the less acid conditions bacteria set to work, other plants invade the habitat, and a true forest embarks upon its infancy. The outcome of this process is that the plant and animal species inhabiting the original biotope either move elsewhere or perish on site. However, owing to topographical changes and post-glacial uplift new bogs originate as old ones are engulfed by the forest. It is therefore possible to envisage a situation in which mobile bog inhabitants, ranging over local areas, come into contact with habitats more favorable than the changing one they were born into. In the case of butterflies, for instance, such movement tends to be passive since an insect does not wilfully move on to greener pastures well beyond the range of its senses. It may be sufficient for survival of a population that a single impregnated female is borne on a favorable wind to a new bog somewhere close by. But if this change to forest should happen too quickly, the whole population may perish in its original home.

What butterflies do in fact inhabit these peat bogs of the taiga zone? Several families are represented, but it is convenient to consider two adaptational groups. Those of the first group complete their life-cycles within one calendar year, while those of the second take two years in order to reach maturity.

By the end of May the first green 'mouse-ears' of leaves have appeared on the birches and, as the cynics (and field workers!) have it, White Winter is ready to give way to Green Winter. In a forward year the cloudberry will already be putting out its white strawberry-like blossoms, one at the end of each stem. From gnarled chrysalids hanging under twigs and dried leaves emerge the first males of Freiya's fritillary. The species' flight time is short, but for four or five days you can, if you are lucky enough to find the right bog, observe these males flying rapidly in typical fritillary fashion on the wetter parts of the bog where the spring melt-water has accumulated. They are soon joined by their females and the orange eggs of these are laid on debris near the cloudberry leaves which form the caterpillars' diet. Two important requirements of this species are, therefore, cloudberry plants and an open, very wet area over which to fly.

Close on the heels of Freiya's fritillary, and often on the same bog, follows Frigga's fritillary. It is slightly larger than its relative but has similar habits, makes use of the same foodplant, and also hibernates as a caterpillar. Frigga's fritillary may be glimpsed skimming up and down wet areas of a bog during the second week of June. By that time the Arctic bog fritillary has put in an appearance. Its underside is one of the most colorful in a

**Female moorland clouded yellow, an attractive 'white' butterfly, is found in the peat bogs of the European taiga. Its green caterpillar hibernates beneath the snow**

picturesque set, as you will probably agree should you be watching one lay its pale yellow eggs on the underside of a leaf of bog whortleberry. An interesting 'white' has a similar interest in this small bush. This is the moorland clouded yellow, whose nearest indigenous relatives occur only in the high fells of Lapland. The different-looking sexes fly at great speed and the green caterpillar hibernates beneath the snow.

A small brown butterfly you might confuse with one of the day-flying heath moths is the large heath butterfly. Its foodplant is any of a variety of thin-leaved sedges, a group of plants which somehow always seems to find a footing in a boggy place. By the time the pale larva has crawled from its egg the final fritillary will have taken wing. This is aptly named the cranberry fritillary, for that tiny creeping plant with the juicy red berries is its larval food. The cranberry fritillary does not seem unduly put off by lack of moisture and when a bog has been artificially dried out you can still sometimes see it hawking up and down as though it had not a care in the world. It disappears, however, with the cranberry.

Named after the same plant is the pretty cranberry blue, which is not entirely dependent upon bogs for its larva will also eat the flowers of bilberries and whortleberries.

The butterflies forming the second group must be regarded as Ice-Age relics. What neater answer to severe springs and falls and short, cool summers than to extend one's growing period over two seasons? Interestingly, the two Finnish bog 'browns', the Baltic grayling and Lapland ringlet, are on the wing in alternating years. The odd years are 'Embla years' while the even years are 'Jutta years' (from their scientific names). Both fly only over pine bogs and have a habit of flitting ghostlike (in negative!) round the stunted trunks, to disappear rather suddenly. It is difficult to approach them without frightening them away but just occasionally you can spot one sitting motionless on the bark, its wings cleverly tilted at such an angle that their shadow is minimal. Exactly, in fact, like the famous grayling but with a pine tree under it instead of a stone or sandy patch.

They are eaters, in the caterpillar stage, of sedges and cotton grass, but the final butterfly of this group brings us back to the broad green, serrated-edged leaves of the cloudberry.

Many bogs in Finland are criss-crossed by ditches (top left) to aid the process of drying out, and thus afforestation. However, afforestation inevitably spells the end of the interesting bog communities of plants and animals. An even more severe threat to the Finnish bogs is the government sponsored extraction of peat for fuel (bottom left). This is not economic, and creates a biological wasteland in the process.

A general view (right) shows a pine bog with cloudberry, bog whortleberry, and bog rosemary; the exposed peat is debris from ditching operations

This is the northern grizzled skipper, a butterfly so rare in southern Finland I have only ever seen one individual flying. It is another of those species which favor very wet situations within the confines of the bog.

Like all insects, these butterfly species are specifically adapted to certain environmental conditions. Their very exacting requirements include the right degree of moisture and they thus disappear from any bog which for one reason or another starts to dry out.

The pine bog community unfortunately has one great failing: it does not grow enough wood to be considered productive land by human beings. The answer is either to let it be, or to artificially drain off the water so as to hasten the afforestation process. Needless to say, it is the latter course that is proving increasingly attractive to landowners. In fact, an organization known as TAPIO has been in existence for several decades. One of its aims is the artificial drying of bogs to yield more wood. A free 'ditch-planning' service is made available to farmers (who own sixty per cent of the country's forest), though the actual cost of implementation – in this case fortunately – must be borne by the landowner. In certain districts the system has been so successful that few ditch-free bogs now exist: in the Tampere area, for instance, only one quarter (40,000 hectares or 98,800 acres) remain to be treated. Ditching over the whole country has already amounted to 2.7 million hectares (6.7 million acres).

Money is the root of much anti-conservation evil and an estimated 15 million extra Finnmarks ($4 million, or £2.3 million) are coming to farmers of the Seinäjoki district within the next few years. This represents an increased production of 250,000 cubic meters of felled wood, or in biological terms, 250,000 more hectares (620,000 acres) of dried-out peat bogs. Nationally, wood exports have gone up by ten times during the last seven years. Associated with this, the country's standing wood has approximately doubled.

One of the supporting, or secondary, reasons, given for ditching is the resulting increase in bilberries, whortleberries, and edible fungi. All of these are gathered in quantities by Finns, yet annually millions of kilos remain unpicked. Why, therefore, attempt to increase these natural products, especially when cloudberries and cranberries, both much in favor and yet available in far smaller quantities, are among

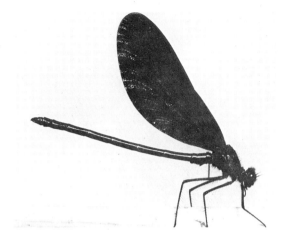

The ditching operations may mean the end of the bogs in the long term, but they do benefit some water-loving insects in the short term, such as the damselfly (top) and the pond skater (above). One of the first butterflies to appear in the Finnish summer is Frigga's fritillary (right), which skims up and down wet, boggy areas in the second week of June

the first things to disappear from the drying bog?

Of all the hastily contrived schemes to emerge as a result of the 1973 'Energy Crisis', the decision of the Finnish government to increase peat-extraction must surely rank among the least sensible. Two or three decades ago the state financed an operation to consider the feasibility of using peat as fuel for central heating systems. It remained in obscurity until the 1973 crisis, when it was brought to the fore. Since one-third of Finland's land area is boggy, many people were firmly convinced that an everlasting supply of fuel could be produced by these 'wasted' areas. Today signposts reading VAPO (State Fuel Organization) can be discovered in previously inaccessible places leading to extensive peat bogs of great biological importance. The incredible thing is that technologists and economists are still firmly convinced that the annual production of peat is unaffected by depredations involving total removal of the upper, productive layer! And in terms of the energy budget, it is not economical to transport the processed peat farther than 100 kilometers from the extraction site, even by rail.

Lack of local literature is a serious handicap to Finnish conservationists. Printing and other taxes are high and the language is understood by less than five million people. Thus even such basic details as those relating to insect life-cycles are often impossible to discover in print. My recent paper on the life-cycle of Freiya's fritillary placed the details on record, yet I cannot believe this species has never before been bred in Finland. Coupled with this dearth of information there has been a serious lack of awareness among the public with respect to environmental matters. Insects, for example, have always been thought of as being either 'useful' or 'harmful', just as land has been considered 'productive' or 'wasteland'.

Television has done something towards setting such matters right. For example, Helsinki University's recently appointed Professor of Environmental Conservation during a television interview in a program devoted to energy problems clearly put across to viewers the concept of the bog being an important source of atmospheric moisture and therefore a habitat of the most useful kind by anybody's standards. Natural history articles have been appearing more often in the press, whilst exhibitions have catered for wildlife photographers. Jorma Luhta's outstanding exhibition 'The cranes are not coming back' focussed attention on the country's rapidly disappearing bog habitats so necessary for survival of the migratory cranes, and it is soon to appear in book form.

But the conservation movement, in all its forms, is far behind the landowners. Only 58,000 hectares (143,318 acres) of the wetter kind of bogs have been declared conservation areas. Some 232,000 hectares (573,000 acres) are 'on the books', but of these 150,000 hectares (370,000 acres) are in private hands. Their purchase would cost the state 130 million marks ($35 million or £20 million). Meanwhile, the bogs dry out and butterfly populations decline.

**The pretty cranberry blue is named after the plant of the same name. It is not entirely dependent on the bogs, for its larvae will also feed on bilberry and whortleberry**

# HABITATS

## ALASKA'S MAGNIFICENT McKINLEY NATIONAL PARK

Erwin Bauer

Before the end of 1978, perhaps as this is being read, the Congress of the United States must decide, once and for all, the future of the largest wilderness – except for Antarctica – left on earth. That wilderness is in Alaska, a lonely land so vast and for the most part so sparsely inhabited that it is hard to comprehend. But today it is threatened with development and exploitation – even pillage – and if any part of Alaska is to be preserved intact for the future, it must be done now.

In 1971, Congress passed into law an Alaska Native Claims Act which required the study of 80 million acres (equivalent to the size of Scandinavia) of public domain to determine if it qualified for national parks, forests, for wild-life refuges, or for wild and scenic rivers. More recently the Secretary of Interior recommended to Congress that 83.5 million acres be included in these four national systems. Environmentalists can only hope that the politicians decide wisely – at least more wisely than they usually do on conservation matters.

The Interior Secretary's proposal includes three new national parks: Lake Clark, Wrangell-St Elias, and Gates of the Arctic, all of these being very large. The Secretary also proposes to increase substantially the size of Mount McKinley, now the only national park in the state, by adding parcels of land well beyond both the north and south boundaries. It is an addition desperately needed for the best administration of the park and its incomparable wildlife.

The proposed addition on the north side of the park would add critical habitat for wildlife – for moose, wolves, and especially caribou. These splendid, easily visible animals are what attract most visitors every summer when the park is open. A large enough southern addition would bring the entire massif of Mount McKinley (at 20,320 feet the highest peak in North America) within the park, which it is not now. It would also add spectacular glacial rivers and brooding, forgotten valleys into the permanent protection of the national park system.

McKinley Park is situated in the heart of an immense wild area near the center of the Alaska Range. Present park boundaries enclose about 7,846 square kilometers, making it America's second (to Yellowstone) biggest national park. When the US Congress established McKinley in 1917, it had ample reason to do so. Beside the almost indescribable grandeur of the landscape, the park was home to thirty-seven species of mammals, 132 species of birds, and more than 400 species of wildflowers, other plants, and trees. Two of the mammals, the barren ground caribou and Dall sheep, cannot be seen in any other park, except Kluane in Canada.

Late in the spring of 1923 the first visitor accommodations were built near the east (and only) entrance to the park. During that first summer only thirty-four intrepid travellers journeyed to McKinley and they could venture no farther than nineteen kilometers by horse and on foot to where a narrow gravel trail dead-ended at Savage River. Because the weather is so often overcast, many of the pioneer tourists

**Moose are usually the first animals spotted by the visitor on entering Mount McKinley National Park, as they are quite tolerant of humans and thus fairly often seen**

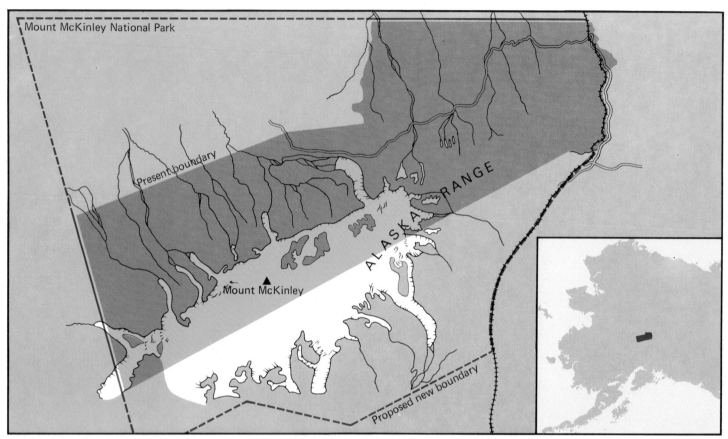

never even had a glimpse of Mount McKinley itself. For several decades, in fact until after World War II, tourism barely existed. Nowadays the number of visitors reaches into six figures during each short summer season, but compared to other American national parks is still only a small number.

I first visited McKinley in 1950 and even at that late date, just twenty-seven years ago, it was almost a pioneering adventure. The seemingly endless drive from the United States–Canada border northward to Alaska and finally to McKinley Park required ten days one way. The abrasive gravel surface of the road, sometimes dusty and sometimes (following summer squalls) a quagmire, devoured tires and broke windscreens. Once beyond southern Canada, there were few accommodations along the way and the only alternative was to pause and pitch a tent when night fell. That was no real hardship, however, except that most campsites were already occupied by swarms of mosquitoes, but few other campers.

By far the most terrible stretch of road was the Denali Highway that meandered over tundra and moraines between Paxson Junction and McKinley Park. In places it was impossible

**Mount McKinley, in Alaska, is set in one of North America's (and the world's) last wilderness areas. It is a land of spectacular scenery and incomparable wildlife. McKinley is grizzly bear country (above), so the visitor does well to use caution to avoid walking into one**

to drive faster than ten or fifteen kilometers an hour. But for 150 miles I encountered only four other cars and the Alaskan bush scenery was magnificent. Along the way I watched my first herd of caribou crossing just ahead, saw willow ptarmigan dusting at the roadside, and watched a long-tailed jaeger catch an Arctic ground squirrel. I also easily caught enough Arctic grayling for dinner from a small ice-cold stream which seemed to originate in snowfields and which had no name on my map.

Then, as now, the only road across McKinley Park itself was the 137-kilometer-long gravel highway, which is still mostly unpaved, and which wandered from the east entrance near the Nenana River to Wonder Lake and Kantishna, a ghost mining town (for gold) just outside the park. Next to the great mountain itself, Wonder Lake is the park's best known landmark; it is the same placid body of water on which McKinley is mirrored in countless familiar photos, on post cards and calendars.

The first animal I encountered once inside McKinley Park was a lynx, a fairly common cat there, but one that is not often seen. Most visitors first spot moose, which are far more tolerant of humans and therefore far more

visible. Early in the season, say June, moose will be grazing or wading in ponds close to that one park road, the females escorted by their ungainly reddish calves and the giant bulls with velvet on their still small antlers. Toward the tag-end of the season, late August or the first two weeks of September before snows close the park, the bulls will have huge palmated antlers, whitened at the tips. They will be restless, moving about, looking for other males to challenge and cows to mate. This is a good time of year for photographers to rely upon telephoto lenses (rather than approaching too close on foot) for moose closeups.

McKinley, I quickly found, was an ideal place to shoulder a light rucksack or daypack, fill it with lunch, binoculars, plenty of film, a foul weather parka, and go hiking for the day across country. Every day thus spent produced exciting experiences I will never forget. It is grizzly bear country, for one thing, and a wise hiker will constantly watch where he is walking to avoid possible confrontation.

During my first trip, and on later visits as well, I have spent much time following and photographing the white Dall sheep which live high along McKinley's thin green ridges. Just getting within camera range is fascinating because it takes you to lofty, lonely places where the only other footprints are of hoofed wildlife. Although it is never an easy climb to within camera range of the sheep, the animals are not overly wary because they have not been hunted by man. A photographer not in a hurry, who makes no sudden moves or strange noises, can gradually become acquainted with most of McKinley's Dall sheep. The ewes with small lambs are the shyest. Some encounters with sheep have been very dramatic and I recall one day in particular.

Early that morning high above Igloo Creek I spotted a band of sheep in a distant and much higher meadow. All were bedded down and I could detect the heavy horns which identified the sheep as adult rams. Right away I filled a rucksack with photo equipment and headed slowly upward in their general direction. It was a very steep ascent.

For about an hour, during which a light drizzle began and soon stopped, I climbed steadily. When I reached a range of about fifty meters, two of the ten rams became slightly uneasy and stood up. While I focused through a 500 mm telephoto lens, the rest arose, stretched, and began to drift away. They were not exactly alarmed, but something about my appearance or approach had disturbed them. Then suddenly I noticed that one ram, the largest of all, did not move away with the others. Instead it stood uncertainly, staring dully at me, as I walked closer and closer. When I stopped and looked through the viewfinder again, I realized I was watching the most magnificent mountain sheep I had ever met anywhere before. At the same time I also realized why the animal showed so little fear. It was too old and too tired to move much – to try to escape – anymore. That great white ram had barely survived the bitter winter just finished and now was living out its last days. I backed slowly away to leave it in peace, but knew that wolves or a grizzly would soon find it.

On still another day I had located sheep and since it was sunny, but threatening, I hurried up a steep slope as fast as my legs would carry me to take advantage of the bright light for photography. All the while grizzly bears were on my mind because I had spent the day before filming a sow with twin cubs. So I was even more than usually careful to avoid bears.

Half way to the sheep, I saw the chance to make a shortcut both in time and distance by crossing rather than circling a deep gully overgrown with willows. A clear game trail led down into the tangle and out the other side. With only the sheep above me in sight, I dropped down into the gully . . . which suddenly seemed to explode. Only a few meters away a large gray brown animal crashed out of the willows just ahead. Several seconds passed before I realized it was a caribou, rather than a grizzly bear, but nonetheless my knees felt liquid – at least too liquid to continue the climb without a long pause.

Until both the mountain and the park were named after a US President who never saw Alaska and had little concern for it, the continent's highest summit was known by several Indian names: Traleika, Trolika, and Denali. The last was used most frequently by Indian tribes of the Yukon, Tanana, and Kuskokwim river regions and today there is great pressure to change the name officially from McKinley to Denali, which means 'the great one' or 'the highest one'.

It is possible that a Russian explorer, Alexei Ilich Chirikof, was the first European to see Denali when he arrived in Alaska in 1741. But it is very unlikely because few Russians wandered far inland and almost none were interested in the immense natural beauty. The first specific mention of the mountain was made by the sea navigator Captain George Vancouver. While surveying Knik Arm of Upper Cook Inlet in 1794, he noted on the distant northwestern horizon that there were 'stupendous mountains covered with snow and detached from one another'. These were mounts McKinley and Foraker, which Captain James Cook failed to sight when he discovered Cook Inlet sixteen years earlier. Bad weather often obscures both peaks for weeks at a time.

The first known map to show McKinley peak was based on information gathered by Baron Ferdinand von Wrangell (for the Russian–America Company) and was published in 1839 in St Petersburg. It is curious that later and generally more accurate maps of Alaska did not show the two mountains. In fact the official Russian map, used as the basis for selling Alaska to the United States in 1867, left the entire area that is today McKinley Park as a complete blank.

However William H. Dall, the first American explorer to view Denali, did so during an

Arctic ground squirrels (above) are numerous and allow the photographer to approach within very close range before moving away. Other wildlife that is often seen includes the snowshoe hares, the almost unbelievably tame red foxes and their kits, and of course wolves (right)

expedition up the Yukon River by skin boat in 1847. He was accompanied by Frederick Whymper, brother of the first man to climb Switzerland's Matterhorn. Many explorations soon followed American possession, some outfitted by the government and others by private enterprises, but it remained for gold prospector William A. Dickey to estimate Denali's elevation with remarkable accuracy and to declare it the highest place on the continent.

The first ascent of McKinley now seems almost fictional – if not downright impossible. It began with a barroom bet in Billy McPhee's saloon in Fairbanks and ended when a party of sourdough miners lugged a four-meter spruce flagstaff, ten centimeters in diameter, to the top in 1910. They undertook the climb without any previous climbing experience, without ropes, with little food, inadequate clothing, in fact without any of the most essential gear on which mountain climbers depend today for less formidable ascents. At the time nobody believed the men had actually accomplished it, but later climbers found their spruce pole and tattered flag on top.

But 1906 proved to be the most important year for McKinley. That was when Charles Sheldon, a prominent big-game hunter and naturalist, spent forty-five days in the present park area, pursuing and studying the wildlife. He was so impressed with his 'discovery' that he returned to spend the winter in McKinley. Later, when chairman of the Boone & Crockett Club (of big-game trophy-hunters) of New York, Sheldon began a personal crusade to have McKinley declared a national park. On 26 February 1917 he personally carried the park bill (which would officially end all hunting) to President Woodrow Wilson's desk for signature. The Boon & Crockett Club had played a major role in the park's establishment and later in other conservation matters as well.

Many more naturalists, some to become celebrated, followed Sheldon to McKinley both for serious research and for the unique wilderness experience of such a magnificent part of the world. Perhaps best known were the brothers Olaus and Adolf Murie who began extensive studies of mammals and birds for the US Biological Survey just after World War I. In July 1923, while concentrating on the bird-life, Olaus made ornithological history when he found the first nest of a wandering tattler ever to be discovered anywhere.

Adolf Murie remains best known for his remarkable studies of the then controversial timber wolf–Dall sheep relationship which he conducted from a log cabin summer home overlooking the Toklat River. He trudged thousands of miles over muskeg and tundra for his intimate observations of both species. I once visited Murie there and met him on field hiking trips. Murie's detailed notes collected during these trips were published in a classic wildlife study, *The Wolves of Mount McKinley*, in 1944 and were reprinted later. The study revealed that wolf predation has a salutary effect on McKinley's Dall sheep population, rather than vice-versa, and that the two species do live in harmony there.

I have been fortunate enough to explore a good many of the finest and best known national parks and wildlife sanctuaries around the world. Very, very few of them (and none in Europe or the New World) offer a visitor such a splendid chance to watch wildlife, natural and unafraid, in such an unpolluted, undisturbed wilderness environment as in McKinley Park. I have already mentioned the moose and caribou which might be seen wandering anywhere. Caribou migrations tend to be erratic and unpredictable, but usually in June and July it is possible to watch vast herds of them travelling parallel to the one park road.

Except very early and very late in the brief summer season, wolves are not easy to spot. But there is always an opportunity unmatched anywhere else. Drive slowly or take the shuttle bus through Sable and Polychrome passes and it is a rare day that grizzly bears are not seen, often near the roadside. Many of McKinley's bears are blonde or sand-colored (locally called Toklats) and therefore easier to identify at a distance than the darker grizzlies elsewhere.

For Dall sheep it is only necessary to look upward near the center of the park to watch for the telltale white figures in high places. Sometimes it is hard to separate them from lingering patches of snow, so a pair of field glasses comes in handy here as well as for watching birds. The hoary marmots of Polychrome Pass permit photographers to stalk very near before they disappear underground, and so do the numerous Arctic ground squirrels. There are snowshoe hares lurking around many of the riverside campgrounds and

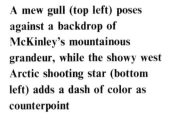

A mew gull (top left) poses against a backdrop of McKinley's mountainous grandeur, while the showy west Arctic shooting star (bottom left) adds a dash of color as counterpoint

108

**The willow ptarmigan, like so much McKinley wildlife, seems tame and unwilling to fly away from the visitor. The park is being extended in two directions, and there is pressure to change its name to the Indian name 'Denali'. But it will still be one of the incomparable spectacles for the wildlife or wilderness enthusiast**

these seem to attract red foxes which are unbelievably tame. On many occasions I have watched (from close at hand, without blinds) foxes hunting ground squirrels and bringing the carcasses to their kits which gamboled around the entrance to the family den.

In contrast to the recent past, McKinley is nowadays an easy park to reach and enjoy. And fortunately this access has been accomplished without compromising the precious wilderness character and atmosphere of the place. Today a good passable road between Anchorage and Fairbanks, Alaska's two main cities, leads directly to the park's only entrance, which is midway between the two. The Alaska Railroad, which runs daily, follows a similar parallel route, also pausing for passengers at the park entrance. A number of motorcoach companies conduct tours of various durations into the park and these probably offer the most comfortable, although certainly not the most thorough, means to see the park and its wildlife.

Auto travel has been severely restricted on the park's single road. Only visitors who have secured reservations in the several public campgrounds along the way are permitted to drive cars as far as their camping destinations. Otherwise all transport is by the free and frequent shuttle buses which will pick up and deposit park visitors wherever they choose. Of course the shuttle bus isn't as convenient as a private car, but its use solves any potential traffic problems.

There is a modest hotel near McKinley's east entrance, as well as other guest houses along the Anchorage–Fairbanks highway out-

side the park. At the west end of the trans-park highway is Camp Denali, a comfortable tented camp which has long been a favorite of serious conservationists and naturalist visitors who relish a wilderness experience while sleeping under canvas. One of the Camp Denali owners, Celia Hunter, is president of The Wilderness Society in the United States.

It is possible to live and travel for a time in McKinley Park by backpacking – or out of a backpack – as many younger visitors do. But such trips should not be considered lightly or be carelessly planned. The weather in central Alaska is damp, often very cold for days on end, a condition which might require periods of confinement in a light tent. Also mosquitoes are apt to be a dreadful nuisance during the middle of the summer (June and July) and any camper must be prepared to cope with them, both mentally and chemically with repellants. My own favorite season is the lovely, golden autumn.

But on those glorious long days when the sun does shine – and during late June it does not really set at all – there are few more exquisite places on this planet than McKinley Park. That is doubly true in the mornings and evenings when there is a strange yellow glow over everything. Denali looms and glistens surrealistically above the scene and grizzly bears wade belly-deep in pink and purple wildflowers. It is indeed an extraordinary place for wildlife watchers – or any others who love the last undisturbed wildernesses.

# WILDLIFE AND CONSERVATION IN THE HAWAIIAN ISLANDS

Bryan Sage

Charles Darwin never visited Hawaii, which is a pity because in terms of the evolution of species in isolation, the Hawaiian islands surpass those of the Galapagos in interest. This is hardly surprising since they are the most isolated islands in the world, lying as they do in the central Pacific Ocean about 2,500 miles from Los Angeles and very nearly 4,000 miles from Japan. Darwin evidently recognized the probable importance of Hawaii since he is said to have offered £50 ($85) to any naturalist who would do some work there.

The Hawaiian islands are quite diverse in character, varying from small and low to large and mountainous. However, there is one feature that they all have in common, and that is their volcanic origin. The islands as seen today are the tall exposed peaks of a series of volcanic submarine mountains strung out along the floor of the Pacific on what geologists term the Hawaiian Ridge. The chain of islands extends for some 1,900 miles on a south-east to north-west alignment. The larger, inhabited, and mostly mountainous islands are in the south-east, and the most interesting of the smaller, sandy, and uninhabited islands are in the north-west. The latter comprise the Hawaiian Islands National Wildlife Refuge and are managed by the United States Federal Fish and Wildlife Service. On the extreme north-west islands of Midway and Kure Atoll are small, mostly military communities.

The evolutionary importance of the Hawaiian islands is evident when we look at the number of species in the fauna and flora that are endemic to the islands. There are no families of plants endemic to Hawaii, but of the approximately 1,381 species of native flowering plants found there, no less than 96.6 per cent are endemic. It is considered that these have evolved from no more than some 275 original immigrant species. In the case of the insects, the 3,722 native species probably evolved from only 250 original immigrants. Equally interesting are the 1,064 species of native land molluscs which could have evolved from as few as two dozen original immigrant species.

The sixty-seven species and subspecies of birds endemic to Hawaii are believed to have evolved from only fifteen original immigrant species. The endemic species of land and freshwater birds are in twenty-five genera, and comprise forty-four species and twenty-three subspecies in eleven different families. This includes twenty-three species and seventeen subspecies of honeycreepers (Drepanididae), a family that is unique to Hawaii.

Unfortunately, the Hawaiian islands have suffered tremendous biotic degradation. At the present time the islands contain a quarter of all endangered fauna in the United States. Of fifty-two types of bird considered endangered by the Department of the Interior, no less than twenty-nine (fifty-six per cent) are endemic to these islands. At the time of the first European contact in 1778 there were sixty-seven types of endemic birds. Since that date no fewer than twenty-three of these have become extinct, and twenty-nine are considered to be endangered, including for example the Hawaiian goose or nene, and the Hawaiian stilt. In fact, more birds have become extinct in Hawaii than in any other area of the world, with the possible exception of the Mascarene islands.

The situation is particularly critical in the case of the honeycreepers, of which no less than fourteen species and subspecies are now extinct, and a further sixteen are classed as endangered. What must surely be one of the most extraordinary ornithological events ever concerns the now extinct Laysan honeycreeper. This bird was confined to Laysan Island where, in a period of two decades up to 1923, introduced rabbits had destroyed the vegetation and turned the island into a virtual desert. In 1923 an American biological survey team visited the island and found that there were only three of these honeycreepers alive – and they were killed in a sandstorm whilst the team were still on the island. The scientists thus had the sad experience of actually witnessing the extinction of a species in the wild.

This high rate of extinction is a sad loss to

A nene or Hawaiian goose in its natural habitat on Maui Island, Hawaii. Having reached a low point of about fifty birds in 1944, it was bred in captivity until some could be released in the islands. There are now thought to be more than 600 on the islands of Maui and Hawaii

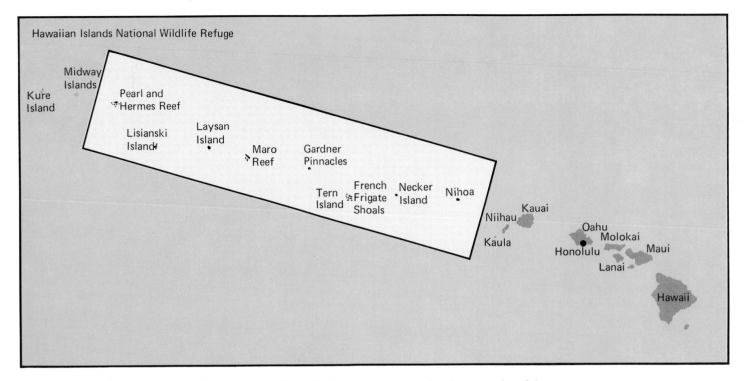

Hawaiian Islands National Wildlife Refuge

Kure Island • Midway Islands • Pearl and Hermes Reef • Lisianski Island • Laysan Island • Maro Reef • Gardner Pinnacles • Tern Island • French Frigate Shoals • Necker Island • Nihoa • Niihau • Kaula • Kauai • Oahu • Honolulu • Molokai • Lanai • Maui • Hawaii

science, particularly as we are still ignorant of the breeding biology of many of the endemic Hawaiian birds. The problem of extinction and endangered populations also exists in other groups, and the only two species of mammal endemic to the islands – the Hawaiian monk seal, and the Hawaiian hoary bat – have both declined to dangerously low populations. A very sad state of affairs exists in relation to the unique Hawaiian land-snail fauna, and of forty-one named species in the genus *Achatinella*, which is confined to the island of Oahu, fourteen are now extinct and another twenty-five are endangered.

The present unfortunate state of much of Hawaii's wildlife and habitats is very largely attributable to the colonization of the islands by man, particularly the white man, and to the relatively recent dramatic increase in the population of the islands. The physical effects of these events are only too well known and include the draining of wetlands, the destruction of native rainforest for agricultural purposes, and urban development. Some of the worst effects of these activities are to be found on the island of Oahu where some eighty per cent of the human population lives, and where the state capital of Honolulu is situated. On Oahu, as on some of the other inhabited islands, the coastal areas in particular have suffered from intensive development.

Oahu represents a classic example of how, in the relatively short time span of 200 years, man can almost totally destroy most of the original vegetation cover of an island, and cause the extinction or near extinction of a considerable proportion of its fauna and flora. Examples of a similar nature can, of course, be found on other islands in the Pacific and elsewhere. What is particularly sad about Hawaii is that so much of a unique nature has been destroyed before it had been properly studied and recorded.

In addition to the physical changes already mentioned, equally serious ecological changes have resulted from the numerous introductions made by man, either accidentally or deliberately. When the first Polynesian settlers arrived about 1,200–1,500 years ago they brought with them the red jungle fowl, dogs, pigs, and the Polynesian rat, as well as various food and fiber plants, weeds, and an unknown number of insects. The magnitude of plant introductions alone is quite startling, and since 1778 over 2,000 kinds of new plants have been introduced to the islands either deliberately or accidentally.

However, the changes caused by the early introductions were insignificant compared to what took place after the arrival of the Europeans, who brought sheep, cattle, horses, goats, and pigs. Later other animals such as

**Alakai Swamp on Kauai Island is the wettest place on earth. Nevertheless two birds—the small Kauai thrush and the Kauai oo—were rediscovered there in the early 1960s**

deer and many birds were introduced to provide hunting. Both brown and black rats also arrived on the scene.

The effect that some of these alien introductions have had on both the island habitats and their associated fauna and flora is not difficult to envisage, and is often only too obvious. Earlier this century some Laysan rails and Laysan finches were transplanted to Midway Island in an effort to establish additional breeding stocks. Due to the depredations of rats none of these birds survived, and the rail is now extinct. The Laysan finch survives on Laysan Island, and on Pearl and Hermes Reef where they had also been transplanted. There is little doubt that the rats are important predators of the nests of both seabirds and of forest birds such as the honeycreepers. I have seen black rats active in the rain forest at 3,500 feet on the island of Kauai, where they probably prey on the eggs and young of tree-nesting honeycreepers and other birds.

In addition to their depredations on birds, the rats also became a serious pest in the sugarcane plantations. A well-meant but misguided attempt to control them was made in 1883 with the introduction of the small Indian mongoose. Unfortunately the mongoose has not succeeded in exterminating the rats, but has itself become a serious predator of the native ducks and geese.

Another introduction that became a serious pest of crops was the giant African land snail. In order to control this the predatory Florida snail was introduced. Unfortunately this idea also misfired in that the Florida snail not only attacked the African land snail, but also moved into the native rain forest habitat where it preyed on the unique Hawaiian species of terrestrial molluscs! This, and the collection of the small exquisitely colored species for the manufacture of earrings, has caused a serious decline in the populations of these native species. Habitat destruction has helped to aggravate the situation. A species of bramble, *Rubus lucidus*, introduced from Florida had become a pest by 1960 and has spread into extensive areas of the native forest.

Despite intensive control measures, feral goats, pigs, and sheep still occur in large numbers on some of the islands. The damage caused by the grazing activities of these animals can be seen quite easily, and their destruction of the vegetation cover often leads to widespread soil erosion. Even in the high altitude rain forest on the island of Kauai, for example, one can see extensive local damage caused by pigs. In the Haleakala Crater area on the island of Maui the damage caused by feral goats is all too evident right up to the crater rim at 10,000 feet. Due to the rugged nature of the terrain on many of the islands, control measures are difficult to implement, and the high rainfall in some areas does not help. In the vicinity of Mount Waialeale on the island of Kauai, the normal average rainfall is 490 inches, but can exceed 600 inches. The extent of the problem can be envisaged from just one report alone, which estimated that from 1921 until 1946 some 10,000 introduced mammals were killed each year in the forest reserves on the island of Hawaii. Some introductions have had less obvious adverse consequences, as for example the Asiatic toad and the so-called cane toad. The latter was introduced from South America to help control pests of the sugarcane plantations.

Despite what has been said so far, all is not entirely gloomy. Nothing can be done about those species that have already become extinct, but there is now a great awareness on the part of both Federal and State authorities of what needs to be done to save the remnants of Hawaii's unique fauna and flora. The remote uninhabited islands that form the Hawaiian Islands National Wildlife Refuge are very important in this context since they support the only remaining populations of some bird species, and provide sanctuary for breeding monk seals. The survival of some bird species is very finely balanced and a good example is the Laysan duck. This is found only on the island of Laysan where 287 were counted in August 1976. They survive on Laysan because that island has a large freshwater lagoon, and it is the absence of this specialized habitat on other islands that precludes any transplant operations.

Another species that has been brought back from the verge of extinction is the Hawaiian goose which, in 1944, was estimated to have a population of less than fifty. By that time their range had also been reduced from about 3,000 square miles on the islands of Hawaii and Maui, to only 1,200 square miles on the former. The natural habitat of this interesting goose is the rugged volcanic terrain between about 5,000 and 7,000 feet above sea level. A

The orange trumpet vine (above) may be very beautiful but it is an exotic plant from Brazil, and should not be in Hawaii. Since 1778 over 2,000 kinds of new plants have been introduced to the islands. The Asiatic toad (left) is but one of many alien animals introduced to the islands—but fortunately in this case without obvious adverse results

The Laysan finch still survives
in small numbers, but an
attempt to establish a separate
colony on Midway Island
earlier this century was
unsuccessful due to the
depredations of rats

restoration project was in due course launched, and the first release of captive-reared birds was made on Hawaii in 1960. In 1962 Hawaiian geese reared at the Wildfowl Trust in England were released in their former habitat in the Haleakala Crater on Maui, and in January 1977 I saw a number in that area which, since they were not banded, had presumably bred in the wild. It has recently been estimated that the population of this goose on the two islands has now reached some 600 birds.

One of the most intensive research efforts ever mounted by the Federal Fish and Wildlife Service is now taking place in the Hawaiian islands as part of a nationwide endangered species program coordinated from Washington, D.C. In recent years the endangered species program has fielded in Hawaii nine teams working on twenty-two endangered forest and waterbirds. New refuges have been established or proposed on the islands of Kauai, Oahu, Maui, Molokai, and Hawaii. The National Park Service protects certain species in the Haleakala National Park on Maui, and in the Volcanoes National Park on Hawaii. In addition, state forests and refuges play an important part in habitat protection.

A good deal of the work on endangered species has been concentrated on the honey-creepers and the honeyeaters (Meliphagidae). There were five species in the latter family in Hawaii, but four are already extinct and the remaining species is endangered. The continued survival of many of the species in these two families will depend upon the maintenance of viable areas of the original native forest, particularly the rain forest where the beautiful flowers of trees such as the ohi a-lehua provide food for some species.

Fortunately, there are still some very inaccessible and remote areas of rain forest on some of the islands, and they have been the scene of some exciting events in recent years. Perhaps the most outstanding event of all was the discovery in 1973 of an entirely new kind of honeycreeper in the high altitude rain forest on the north-east slopes of the Haleakala Crater. This bird has been named the po'o uli, and its population is estimated to be only about twenty-five birds, all confined to one valley. Also confined to this general area of forest is the crested honeycreeper which is locally common between 5,000 and 6,000 feet above sea level, but a few of this species may also survive on the island of Molokai. Out of the total of twenty-nine species and subspecies of birds regarded as endangered, no less than ten (four wetland and six forest birds) occur on the island of Kauai. Two of these are species which were believed to be extinct but were rediscovered in the early 1960s in the extremely wet rain forest of the Alakai Swamp area. One of these is the small Kauai thrush, and the other the only surviving species of honeyeater in Hawaii, the Kauai oo. The population of the latter seems to consist of only a few dozen individuals. The size of the remaining thrush population is unknown, but its distribution is restricted to the ohi a-lehua forest of the Alakai Swamp and it appears to be sensitive to changes in its environment. This is one of the birds that could be seriously affected by the spread of alien plant species into the rain forest habitat.

The endangered waterfowl of Hawaii include the Laysan duck and the Hawaiian goose, both of which have been discussed already. Others in this category are the Hawaiian duck, gallinule, coot, and stilt. These birds inhabit the lowland ponds and marshes of the main islands where their preservation is a matter of some urgency, since wetland habitats are being destroyed by draining or infilling. The most numerous of these birds is the Hawaiian duck which may number about 3,000 individuals, almost all of which are located on the island of Kauai. The stilt, on the other hand, although more widely distributed, has a population of probably no more than 1,500 birds. One of the important areas on Kauai for waterbirds is the Hanalei taro fields or paddies which were once very extensive, but now cover about 150 acres and form the Hanalei National Wildlife Refuge where the coot, duck, and stilt all breed. The interesting point about this habitat is that it is entirely artificial and depends upon the practice of taro growing. Taro is used for making a starchy paste that forms an important part of the diet of some of the local people, the cycle of planting to harvesting taking about eighteen months. Ensuring that taro growing continues is part of the management technique for this refuge. At one time rice and taro fields in Hawaii provided over 34,000 acres of wetland habitat, but today such fields comprise only a few hundred acres; that is how serious the situation has become.

The naturalist planning to visit the Hawaiian

The Laysan duck (top) is found only on Laysan Island. It numbers less than three hundred, and depends on the island's freshwater lagoon. But besides its interesting resident species, Hawaii plays host to many non-breeding visitors, especially in the coastal regions. These include the attractive wandering tattler (above)

**The only two native Hawaiian mammals—the monk seal (above) and the hoary bat have declined to dangerously low levels. However, the monk seal is protected during breeding in the Hawaiian Islands National Wildlife Refuge**

islands should not be put off by all these problems. Although strict controls have to be placed on access to many areas such as the refuge islands in the north-west of the chain, and the Kipahulu Valley (the greatest stronghold of endemic plants in Hawaii) on Maui, there is more than enough to see. There are trails through splendid rain forest areas on Kauai which enable one to see many interesting plants and birds, including the commoner species of honeycreeper, and there are visiting arrangements for refuge areas. On Maui the Haleakala Crater is excellent, not only for seeing the Hawaiian goose and other birds, but for its interesting flora and spectacular scenery. One of the most remarkable of the plants is the silversword, a member of the daisy family. It grows on the barren slopes of the old volcanic cones and takes from ten to thirty years before it flowers, at which point it produces a flower spike up to nine feet tall and then dies. An interesting shrub is the rare Haleakala sandalwood with its beautiful red flowers; it is found nowhere else in Hawaii other than this crater. In addition to the resident birds of the islands, there are some interesting non-breeding visitors to be seen, especially in coastal regions. These include the American golden plover, wandering

tattler, and the rare bristle-thighed curlew.

It is to be hoped that the efforts of numerous individuals and the various government agencies to save what remains of Hawaii's unique fauna and flora will meet with success, for it would be a tragedy for science and mankind should any more species pass into oblivion.

# PHUKET ISLAND PARADISE LOST

John A Burton

The island of Phuket is described in the travel agents' brochures as one of the classic paradise isles. And there seems to be more than an element of truth in the description. Phuket is situated in the Andaman Sea, on the Indian Ocean coast of peninsular Thailand, some seven degrees north of the equator. Coconut palms shade wide, sandy beaches, and the island is fringed with coral reefs which swarm with life. The center of the island rises to a height of more than 1,000 feet and the hills are shrouded with luxuriant tropical rain forest vegetation in which lurk exotic birds, arboreal crabs, and flying lizards. In the lowlands water buffalo loll lazily in the *klongs* (canals) which irrigate the rice paddies. Starvation, a feature of so many parts of Asia, must be virtually unknown on an island where practically any fruit or vegetable will grow in a matter of months and where fish, prawns, crabs, and a host of other seafoods are available in incredible abundance.

But beneath the idyllic surface there are undercurrents that are not so benign. For instance, the town of Phuket has three gun shops, one of which I visited. On sale were a variety of rifles, shotguns, and hand guns. There were also hand grenades and factory-made sawn-off shotguns. One cannot know exactly what these arms were intended for – but it seems fair to say that not all of them were for entirely legal practices. A few days before my arrival fifteen people had been killed in a demonstration when a hand grenade exploded accidentally. Hunting, both legal and illegal, is widespread and popular all over Thailand.

Superficially, Phuket is the paradise island that the travel brochures claim, but the longer I stayed the more I came to realize that there were considerable problems in maintaining this particular paradise.

Tourists come to the island and they want to take home souvenirs. In Phuket town itself there are now some sixteen shops supplying souvenirs, in addition to many stalls, shops, and hotels in other parts of the island. These souvenirs include complete turtles, dried crabs and other crustaceans, shells, coral, stuffed animals and a multitude of other wildlife, and gifts made from bits of animals.

The act of collecting such wildlife – particularly that from the coral reefs – usually destroys as much if not more than actually appears on the counter for sale. A collector walking over the reefs searching for molluscs (which will be killed to obtain perfect shells) tramples down the very coral which is their habitat. Corals, particularly rare kinds, are themselves torn out to be dried and bleached for the souvenir trade.

The exploitation of natural resources involved in catering for the tourist market on Phuket is direct and fairly easy to quantify, but there is another equally important form of exploitation – for food. Having indulged myself, I can well understand this, for it really is superb. A large transient population of tourists, paying for the privilege, could unknowingly do untold damage to the local resources, by creating a demand for rarities, as well as putting a considerable strain on the amount of food available.

Tourists also engage in sport fishing, though compared with other threats I doubt that this is significant. However, the sport that has undoubtedly affected the indigenous wildlife is shooting by the local Thais. The Buddhist religion forbids the killing of animals except for food, but many of the people in southern Thailand are Muslims, and even the Buddhists can get round the problem by eating a small piece of meat from their quarry so that they can justify their killings. Hence, with firearms easily available, such birds as hornbills are now being over-hunted.

The effects of tourism on the wildlife and natural environment are certainly significant, but more disastrous to the paradise island are some of the local commercial operations. Firstly, logging (much of it illegal) is rapidly reducing the area of rain forest, and consequently the flora and fauna associated with this habitat. I visited some of the remaining forest in the hills of Phuket and saw spectacular trees,

**Phuket Island, off the west coast of peninsular Thailand, is the classic tropical island, but it is in danger of destroying itself through a combination of commercial interests and tourist pressures. It is unfortunately typical of all too many similar islands**

flying lizards, slow lorises, eagles, hornbills, and a variety of other wildlife. Leaf monkeys, gibbons, and other animals can also be seen. But the encroachment of agriculture and rubber plantations is proceeding at an alarming rate.

One of the side effects of deforestation is that soil runs off into the rivers and even directly into the sea, not only degrading the land but at the same time increasing the amount of silt which is flushed into the ocean. This silt can have a disastrous effect on the reefs, choking and killing the coral. Many of the coral reefs which I saw are now silted over and derelict, yet Dutch engineers working on Phuket remember them being alive and thriving as recently as 1970.

If the silt from the hillsides is bad, then the silt from the mining operations is even worse. Phuket is rich in tin, which is being mined both legally and illegally. The inland tin mines add vast quantities of silt to the rivers, but off-shore dredges are also a problem. The offshore tin dredging operations (in which Dutch and British interests are deeply involved) also produce vast amounts of silt which adds to the general clogging of the coral reefs.

As one might expect, the illegal dredging is on a fairly small scale. But it would be easy to reduce the impact of the legal but very harmful large-scale operations. If dredging were restricted to outgoing tides, instead of twenty-four hours a day, the silting of the coastal areas would be considerably reduced.

A third environmental catastrophe is the destruction of the mangroves. To most people mangroves appear to be wastelands of no use. In fact, they are among the most productive ecosystems in the world. Many of the fish, crabs, prawns, and shellfish which are caught in the sea come to the nutrient-rich waters near the mangroves to breed, and so the sphere of influence of the mangrove spreads far and wide. Unfortunately, mangrove timber makes first-class charcoal. The crabs served in the Phuket hotels are more than likely to be cooked on charcoal from the rapidly disappearing mangroves – which the crabs themselves need in order to reproduce!

Once the mangroves have been cut, the land tends to be drained and turned into rice paddies. Yet if the cutting were more selective and controlled, a high yield of timber for charcoal could be expected because mangrove

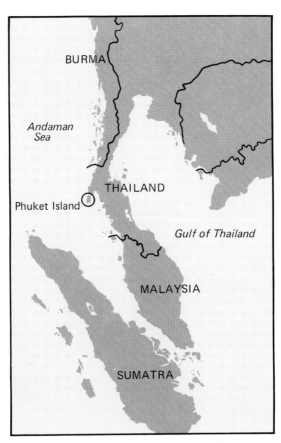

appears to have remarkable powers of regeneration.

So we have on Phuket a classic conflict – Industry versus the Environment. Normally the environment has a weak voice, but in this instance it is of prime importance to a rapidly developing tourist industry. Tourists are not going to visit an island to see rubber plantations and bare hillsides, and derelict reefs are not a pretty sight. Without the fish, shellfish, and other seafoods the cuisine will no longer be an attraction. However, local business interests are obviously involved in the rapid exploitation of the forest and the mineral resources – both of which are short-term.

To the outsider the solution is simple: slow down, strictly control land usage and dredging, and set aside forest reserves. But in the context of a country with quite different values, and where pressure from business interests is not unknown, these objectives may be difficult to achieve.

Phuket is rich in tin, and the inland (above) and offshore mining and dredging operations pour an increasing amount of silt into the sea, thus helping to kill the fringing coral reefs.

Another form of destruction is to be seen in this tourist shop on Phuket (right) which offers a wide variety of merchandise featuring marine molluscs and crustaceans

# ABUKO
# A
# CONSERVATION
# INSPIRATION

Michael Gore

By any standards Abuko Nature Reserve is small, and in the African context it is minute, but the wealth and variety of the flora and fauna it contains and its importance as an inspiration to the conservation effort is out of all proportion to its size.

Abuko Nature Reserve is situated fifteen miles outside Banjul, the capital of The Gambia on the West African coast. The Gambia itself is small, a narrow strip of land averaging fifteen miles wide on either side of the Gambia River and stretching inland for some 300 miles. But despite its size The Gambia is setting an example to other countries in the region by its efforts to conserve the country's remaining wildlife – and Abuko Nature Reserve is the focal point of this movement.

At the time of writing the reserve comprises just 191 acres, though by 1978 it should be nearly doubled in size. A stream flows through a series of pools down the center of the reserve and this is bordered by lush riverine forest; away from the water the vegetation gives way to typical Guinea savanna, and so there is a variety of habitats available which accounts for the abundance of the wildlife.

The reserve contains a representative selection of the smaller West African mammals; there is a breeding herd of the endangered West African race of the sitatunga, numbers of bushbuck, three species of duiker, two of porcupine, and civets, mongooses, and genets. And as recently as 1970 a leopard was regularly reported there. Monkeys abound – both the green vervet and red patas are common but the most spectacular are the troops of graceful western red colobus monkeys which are to be seen moving through the forest canopy, each troop invariably accompanied by one or two magnificent mona monkeys.

Abuko also provides a temporary home for chimpanzees which have been confiscated from illegal traders by the Gambian police. Young chimpanzees are sometimes brought down the Gambia river from Senegal and Guinea for sale in Banjul. Once recovered they are placed in Abuko until they are old enough to be sent to Niokola-Koba National Park in Senegal where there is a chimpanzee rehabilitation station run by a young English girl, Stella Brewer.

Both Nile and dwarf crocodiles are present in the stream and pools; the former may often be observed sunning themselves on the banks but the latter, being mainly nocturnal, are rarely seen. Snakes are common and visitors may see both the large African python and the smaller royal python. One fortunate party recently witnessed a fight to the death between a crocodile and a sixteen-foot African python; inevitably, the crocodile was the victor. Cobras, puff adders, and green mambas are among the other snakes which occur though these are rarely encountered.

It is the birds, however, which are Abuko's special attraction and nearly 180 different species have been recorded there, including some of the most colorful in West Africa: the striking gonolek or barbary shrike, paradise flycatchers, three species of hornbill, four sunbirds, two touracos, and no less than eight species of kingfisher, are all found in Abuko. Many of these and possibly another eighty species may be observed during an afternoon's stroll through the reserve.

Abuko's importance to the conservation movement has been its success both with Gambians and foreign tourists. In the nine years since it was created it has proved to the government the value of wildlife reserves both for educational purposes and as places of interest which visitors must have if the country's developing tourist industry is to expand. Now a large island reserve is planned inland along the Gambia river which will give protection to the hippopotomuses still found there and, in the longer term, a national park into which it is proposed to reintroduce some of the larger animals of the African savanna which are now rare or have become extinct in The Gambia during this century.

However, even when the other reserves are open Abuko will continue to be the focal point of the conservation movement in The Gambia.

**The striking gonolek or Barbary shrike is only one of nearly 180 birds that have been recorded in the Abuko Reserve**

An education center, including a cinema for screening wildlife films, has recently been completed as part of an observatory which overlooks the main crocodile pool and here groups of school children and tourist parties are introduced to the subject and taught how to enjoy the flora and fauna which The Gambia has to offer. Adjoining the reserve the Wildlife Conservation Department headquarters, financed by Britain as part of the aid program to The Gambia, should by now be in use.

The Conservation Education Centre was inaugurated as part of the festivities celebrating the twelfth anniversary of independence, The Gambia's National Day, on 18 February 1977. On that occasion the President, Alhaji Sir Dawda Jawara, made wildlife conservation the main theme of his speech to the country – a brave gesture by a committed man, for a general election was only six weeks away and conservation is not a particularly popular subject with people in developing countries.

President Jawara began his speech by saying: 'It is necessary that all the gifts of nature must be carefully utilized', and went on to talk of the strains imposed on the countryside everywhere as a result of the demand for land for development purposes. 'Human needs must come first,' he said, 'but it is necessary to exercise control over the uses of our resources and not to exploit them indiscriminately.'

The President urged schoolchildren to take an interest in wildlife, and told teachers to foster this interest and encourage pupils in their charge to make the study of wildlife their hobby. He concluded his speech, which was made to a large gathering in the main square of the capital, by reading the Banjul Declaration in which he pledged his government's determination to conserve the country's remaining fauna and flora.

President Jawara is a veterinary surgeon and has a deep interest in wildlife and a personal commitment to conservation. One of the first recommendations in the country's Five-Year Development Plan to be implemented was the establishment, within his Presidential Office, of a Wildlife Conservation and Management Department; Eddie Brewer, father of Stella Brewer, was appointed as the country's first Director of Wildlife Conservation.

Eddie Brewer is no stranger to The Gambia. He first went there in 1958 as Forestry Development Officer, a post he had previously held in

Though small—about 400 acres—the reserve contains a representative selection of West African mammals. These include a breeding herd of the endangered West African race of the sitatunga (above); Grimm's duiker (top left), as well as two other species of duiker, and fair numbers of bushbuck (bottom left). There are also porcupines, civets, mongooses, and genets the Seychelles. In fact, conservation in The Gambia owes much to his efforts during his years as a forester for it was he who, in 1968, established Abuko as the country's first reserve.

With Eddie Brewer heading the Wildlife Conservation Department and with support from the World Wildlife Fund – they have allocated funds to help establish the department and Guy Mountfort, a Trustee of World Wildlife, was present at the 1977 Independence Day celebrations to hand over a mobile education film unit provided – the prospects for conservation in this part of West Africa look bright. It is to be hoped that other countries in the region will emulate the example set by The Gambia whose Wildlife Conservation Act passed by the House of Representatives in March 1977 includes the following clause: 'Save as otherwise provided under this Act, any wild animal found in The Gambia, whether or not originating in The Gambia, shall be a protected animal.'

The gray-headed kingfisher (left) is one of no less than eight different species of kingfisher found in Abuko. The most spectacular monkeys in the reserve are the western red colobus monkeys which move in troops through the forest canopy

(Over page) Male red-bellied paradise flycatcher at its nest; the female's tail is almost as long

# WORLD WILDLIFE FUND REPORT

The year 1977 brought the challenge of saving the seas dramatically before governments and public. There were huge oil spills, including the one from the *Argo Merchant* off Massachusetts, and in the North Sea there was an oil-well blow-out which took a week to control. Neither of these incidents seems to have had such dire consequences as were feared at the time, but only because of a fortunate coincidence of timing and weather conditions. Heavy seas broke up the slicks, which did not seriously touch neighboring shores; seabirds were not in the areas at that time, and fish spawning was not in progress.

Both incidents were apparently due to human error – a ship off course, and an oil well part wrongly fitted. They could have caused tremendous damage to fisheries and the ecology of the seas. There should be no complacency because

they did not. Rather they should be taken as warnings.

At the same time fisheries were making news. In the past our favorite sea foods were usually readily available, and mention of cod, herring, tuna, and other fish seldom featured on the main news pages. Now we have seen Britain and Iceland squabbling over cod fisheries; a long-term ban on herring fishing in the North Sea; and the United States and other nations have put strict controls on others fishing within a 200-mile limit of their shores in order to conserve falling stocks.

Feeling over the continued slaughter of the great whales, mainly by Japan and the Soviet Union, continued to grow stronger as the catches declined, indicating that the whales were becoming fewer.

The international conference on the Law of

the Sea met again and failed to resolve the bitter differences over rights to exploitation of marine resources.

It was in this atmosphere that the World Wildlife Fund began its biggest-ever campaign under the slogan THE SEAS MUST LIVE. This campaign is to raise $10 million for action projects to save the seas and marine resources, worked out by leading world scientists under the auspices of the International Union for Conservation of Nature and Natural Resources (IUCN). The IUCN, and many of the scientists involved, have been working closely with other concerned organizations, principally the United Nations Environment Programme (UNEP), the Food and Agriculture Organization (FAO), and UNESCO.

As Sir Peter Scott, Chairman of the World Wildlife Fund, has said: 'This is rightly the biggest campaign the World Wildlife Fund has undertaken because the threat to the seas, which play a vital role in our lives, is one of the most dangerous we face. We want to harvest food from the seas to feed our exploding human population. But at the same time we pour poisonous industrial effluent into the estuaries and coastal regions, which are often the breeding and feeding grounds of the fish we catch. In many places now the fish are unfit to eat, and deposits of mercury, cadmium and other heavy metals have already taken a human toll.

'Rich fisheries are being over-exploited, using ever more efficient technology, and some have already been reduced below any real commercial importance. Attempts at international control continually founder on the rocks of national greed and intransigence.

'Oil has become one of the bases of our lives, but by careless handling we are letting it damage and destroy sea life – killing seabirds, fouling the shores and suffocating marine organisms. Further lethal damage is done by chemicals like DDT and PCBs.

'Just as on land, wild animals are an index of the health of the seas. Their decline before our very eyes is clear evidence that things are going wrong. What can better illustrate over-exploitation than the tragedy of the whales, the greatest creatures known to have lived on earth? Massive exploitation for oil, meat and whale-bone has reduced their numbers to a mere fraction of what they were. And still hunting continues despite international pleas.

'In catching tuna, hundreds of thousands of dolphins are drowned in the nets. Ways to stop this tragic, criminal waste are being worked out and must be implemented urgently.

'Seals, turtles and sea cows are being persecuted and decimated, and our shorelines are becoming sterile, if not poison-oozing concrete jungles instead of the natural link between land and sea. Let us remember that life began in the seas, from which our distant ancestors emerged to adapt themselves to terrestrial life. How could such an evolutionary process take place today?'

The action program launched by the World Wildlife Fund in 1977 tackles the conservation of critical areas essential for the survival and productivity of food and commercial species, as well as of rare and threatened ones.

Scientists and legal experts began planning the establishment of an international system of sanctuaries for whales, dolphins and porpoises, which would include protection of the calving lagoons used by the gray whale on the Pacific coast of Mexico; a sanctuary for the humpback whale off Hawaii; and for the blue whale – the greatest of all – in the Gulf of the St Lawrence.

Among seals there was special concentration on saving the Mediterranean monk seal, whose scattered population, extending also along the northwest coast of Africa, has been reduced to about 500. The seals of the Baltic and Wadden Sea, which are badly affected by pollution and loss of habitat, also received attention.

The sea cows – dugongs and manatees – which live along the shores of the warm tropical seas and gave birth to the legend of the mermaid, are threatened with extinction because they are easily killed for food, and the seagrass beds on which they graze are being destroyed. Special efforts are being made to establish sound conservation measures.

For the great migrations of wading birds the effort started to establish a 'green route' of protected estuaries and marshes, down the coast of western Europe to Africa. These areas are being polluted or reclaimed because their biological importance is not appreciated.

Other projects involved conservation of the marine otter on the coasts of Chile and Peru; of marine turtles throughout the tropical seas and especially on the shores of Brazil, India, Malaysia, and Pakistan; of coral reefs, destroyed for building materials, souvenirs and jewelry; of molluscs, mangroves and seagrasses.

**A leopard carries off its antelope prey in one of Kenya's national parks**

The World Wildlife Fund is particularly concerned that marine resources should be properly managed to maintain their productivity, and apart from the development and promotion of management programs the campaign includes action to ensure that the proposed international Law of the Seas takes conservation measures fully into account.

The World Wildlife Fund and IUCN joined other conservation organizations in supporting a special ecological and economic study of the Palau archipelago, 500 miles east of the Philippines, to combat proposals by American, Japanese and Iranian interests for a superport and petroleum store for the Pacific area. Such a development would destroy one of the most spectacular and pristine environments in the Pacific and completely change the life of its people. The aim of the study is to present the people of Palau with all the information for them to make their own decision on what their future should be.

The campaign for the seas is occupying the leading place in the World Wildlife Fund's program for at least three years, but at the same time the conservation of terrestrial habitats and wildlife is not being neglected. The tropical rain forests continue to be under assault with over fifty acres a minute falling before the bulldozers and power saws, and being burned away by settlers for cropland, which usually proves of quickly diminishing value. Nearly half the original tropical rain forest area of 6.4 million square miles has already gone.

The tropical rain forests formed a green belt round the center of the earth and, until recently, were the last great ecosystem almost untouched by man. They hold the richest collection of species of animals and plants on the planet, and through the ages have provided valuable drugs, medicines, foods, and other products. Their vast potential to provide more products valuable to man has scarcely been tapped – for example, Chinese scientists recently reported finding a plant producing a substance which can be used as an antifreeze.

The World Wildlife Fund raised over $2 million in 1975–6 in a special tropical rain forest campaign to press forward an IUCN conservation program. Detailed surveys of all the different types of rain forest in south-east Asia, from which were derived recommendations for reserves and rational exploitation,

were followed up in tropical America in 1977, and are being extended to Africa.

Equipment and technical assistance has been provided for parks and reserves in Ghana, Rwanda, and Senegal in Africa; in Brazil, Colombia, Costa Rica, Cuba, Ecuador, Peru, and Venezuela in the Americas; and Indonesia, Malaysia, and Thailand in Asia.

The Indonesian program was of special note, having been established as a joint Indonesian Government and World Wildlife Fund enterprise for which the World Wildlife Fund pledged one million dollars. It consists of seventeen projects to conserve the extremely rich and complex fauna and flora of an area which includes the Malaysian and Australasian faunal regions, with the overlapping area. The growing human population, shifting cultivation, poaching, illegal trade in animals, and various kinds of industrial development, in particular timber exploitation, are the big threats. The program aims at establishing a representative network of reserves containing viable examples of all rain forest ecosystems. Among the animals it is hoped to save from extinction or further depletion are the Javan rhinoceros, now numbering about fifty after touching a low point of twenty in the 1960s; the Javan tiger, which is on the brink with less than five survivors; the Sumatran tiger, which numbers around 800; the orang utan and several species of gibbon; and Kuhl's deer which is found only on the island of Bawean.

An educational program in collaboration with the Indonesian authorities to make ordinary people conservation-minded in their own interests and those of the community as a whole has been launched first of all in Sumatra and will be extended to Java and other islands over the next four years.

In India support was given to the National Committee on Environmental Planning and Coordination for a Task Force report on Ecological Planning for the Western Ghats. This is a chain of forested mountains down the west coast from Bombay which receives the brunt of the monsoon and which plays a vital role in the lives of tens of millions of people in drought-prone areas to the east. The Task Force has made detailed recommendations for the conservation of the Ghats.

Another ecosystem of great importance which is being constantly eroded is the wetland. To the uninitiated, wetlands often appear

**An African elephant photographed by Dr Iain Douglas-Hamilton, director of the World Wildlife Fund's elephant conservation project**

rather barren dull areas, perhaps enlived by a few ducks but otherwise fit for reclamation or dumping. In fact they are exceptionally rich biological areas, and are the key to water supplies and conservation for surrounding areas. No wetland could be more important than the Wadden Sea fringing the Netherlands, Germany and Denmark. This is where nearly all the North Sea herring are nurtured, along with eighty per cent of the plaice and over half of the brown shrimp and sole. This, without mentioning the millions of birds which use and contribute to the wealth of the Wadden Sea, is surely sufficient reason for top priority conservation. However, the poisonous effluent of northwest Europe's industries pouring down the Rhine, the Meuse, the Elbe and the Schelde is allowed to penetrate the Wadden Sea.

The World Wildlife Fund is continuing its support for the Netherlands Society for the Preservation of the Wadden Sea, the Wadden Sea Working Group in Denmark, and a group of local conservation organizations in Germany, and for scientific studies by universities and research institutes. The aid is for equipment for research and public awareness programs; lease of areas where wildlife needs protection and for wardens; and for legal studies. The IUCN has prepared a draft convention on the Wadden Sea which is under discussion by the three countries involved.

Two other great European wetland areas were also objects of World Wildlife Fund attention – the Doñana National Park in the Guadalquivir estuary near Seville, Spain, and the Camargue, the Mediterranean delta of the Rhône. Both face problems of pollution from industrial and agricultural activities which discharge damaging wastes into the rivers. A management plan for the Doñana area was worked out, while a pollution study in the Camargue was supported as a model for application to other estuaries.

The World Wildlife Fund's Italian organization devoted itself to the management of a series of key wetlands on the west coast between Leghorn and Orbetello, which are important waterfowl refuges. Nature trails and exhibitions were developed to educate the public.

Similarly, support was given for wetland reserves managed by the Wildfowl Trust in Britain, and to the Tunisian Government's conservation program for a series of important lakes.

The conservation of habitat is obviously of crucial importance because the survival of individual species depends ultimately upon it. But emergency action is also required to ensure that many animals are not wiped out. Operation Tiger, which covers conservation work in Bangladesh, Bhutan, India, Indonesia, and Thailand, went into its fourth year with encouraging signs that tiger numbers are at least stabilized in most protected places. However with only four or five individuals left there are serious prospects that the Javan tiger will follow the Bali tiger into oblivion. A scientist supported by the World Wildlife Fund has provided the Indonesian authorities with a management plan for the Meru Betiri reserve in eastern Java. The other Indonesian tiger is the Sumatran and surveys were made to establish a reserve. About 800 Sumatran tigers survive, but they are still being heavily hunted despite legal protection.

Another major project which continued was for the conservation of elephants. Despite their size the numbers of elephant are unknown, and the first task is collection of basic data, including distribution. The African elephant may still number about two million but in all but five of the thirty countries in which it is found it is decreasing. The Asian elephant is in an extremely dangerous situation and is estimated to number only between 27,000 and 40,000 in a range from India to south-east Asia.

The breaking up of elephant territory by human settlement creates problems both for elephants and people whose interests clash, and one of the aims of the project is to work out a *modus vivendi*.

The lure of ivory is still one of the biggest threats to elephants, and the World Wildlife Fund's effort is to try to get governments to understand the valuable economic resource represented by their elephant populations, if they protect them. A possible solution would be the establishment of an ivory cartel such as the Diamond Board, which would control ivory exploitation and help to ensure that the community as a whole benefits from this renewable resource.

The graceful vicuña of the high Andes continued to prosper, representing one of the most successful conservation stories. Since protective measures were taken ten years ago, when numbers had been reduced to about 15,000, the vicuña population has more than quadrupled

**A brown grizzly bear in Montana**

and controlled exploitation for the benefit of the impoverished local communities is rapidly becoming a possibility.

The deserts of Arabia have been bereft of the white oryx for many years now, but fortunately the World Wildlife Fund helped capture some of the last wild specimens in 1962. They were taken to the Phoenix Zoo, Arizona, and, together with captive animals, formed the nucleus of a so-called 'World Herd', which has increased to such an extent that reintroduction to protected areas in Arabia is possible. The first place will be the Shaumari reserve in Jordan where the World Wildlife Fund has been helping the Jordanian authorities prepare the necessary facilities. Soon after it is hoped to release oryx again in Oman.

Last ditch attempts were being taken to save several species, notably the pampas deer in Argentina, the Kashmir stag or hangul in India, and the waldrapp ibis in Turkey. Only about 100 of the southern form of the pampas deer survive, split into three locations. The conservation effort is being concentrated mainly on a private ranch south of Buenos Aires where a team of scientists has been taking measures to improve the habitat and the food and water available to the deer.

The hangul, a race of the red deer, winters mainly in the Dachigam sanctuary in Kashmir, and here also one of the top priorities is to ensure proper habitat management to improve the pasture, as well as to prevent poaching.

The waldrapp ibis once bred over large areas of Europe and western Asia but it now nests only on some ledges within the village of Bireçik on the banks of the Euphrates in Turkey. Unfortunately, although local concern about the bird's survival has been aroused, building activities around the nesting area are continuing. An attempt has therefore been started to encourage the birds to adopt a new nesting area outside the village. Only thirteen pairs bred in 1977, producing seventeen fledglings, whereas the colony consisted of 1,300 birds twenty-five years ago.

There was growing concern about the scimitar-horned oryx, for which the Ouadi Rimé-Ouadi Achim Faunal Reserve in Chad is virtually the last refuge. Drought caused a shortage of pasture and the oryx were forced southwards towards populated areas where they are threatened by poaching. Because of the disturbed political situation, patrolling was

greatly restricted, and the project leaders reported that unless protection could be stepped up the oryx could decline below the survival level within five years.

An important facet of the World Wildlife Fund's work is to support key conservation organizations, of which the most important is the International Union for Conservation of Nature and Natural Resources.

The IUCN is the world's leading scientific conservation organization and works in close association with the United Nations Environment Programme (UNEP), the Food and Agriculture Organization (FAO), and UNESCO. Several hundred of the leading world environmental scientists are associated with the IUCN, enabling it to identify conservation needs and priorities and to develop programs, such as that for the seas.

The International Council for Bird Preservation and the International Waterfowl Research Bureau received supporting grants for their work.

As part of the effort to inculcate conservation values in the young, cooperation was maintained with the World Scout Movement, which has been helped to make practical conservation a key part of scouting activities.

In sum, the year 1977 saw no lessening of the threats to the natural world. Indeed many became more acute. However the World Wildlife Fund was encouraged by the fact that both governments and the public showed a growing awareness of the environmental crisis and the need for action. It is crucial that all should realize that conservation is not a barrier to progress and development, but an essential part of the management of the world's natural resources on which we are utterly dependent.

**A killer whale leaps out of the water off Vancouver Island**

# BOARD OF TRUSTEES

**Members of the Board of Trustees of the World Wildlife Fund**
*President* John H. Loudon*
*Chairman* Sir Peter Scott*
*Executive Vice-President* Dr Luc Hoffman*
*Honorary Treasurer* Louis Frank*

*Members*
Syed Barbar Ali
Robert O. Anderson
Mrs Thomas J. Bata*
Felipe Benavides
Dr Harold J. Coolidge
Miss Fleur Cowles
Chief S. L. Edu
Irving J. Feist
Eskander Firouz
Claude Foussier
Professor Dr Rudolf Geigy
Professor Dr Bernhard Grzimek
John W. Hanes Jr
Dr Thor Heyerdahl
Baroness Jackson of Lodsworth
Axel Axe:son Johnson
Dr Francisco Kerdel Vegas
Mrs Samuel Koechlin-Smythe
General P. P. Kumaramangalam
Dr Albert Löhr
The Hon. Alan A. Macnaughton
Mrs Robert A. Magowan
Professor Dr H. C. Manfred von Mautner Markhof
Jose M. Mayorga*
Guy Mountfort*
H.R.H. Princess Beatrix of the Netherlands
A. W. Nielsen
Sir Arthur Norman
David Ogilvy*
Dr Aurelio Peccei
Professor Jacques Piccard
Professor S. Dillon Ripley
J. MacLain Stewart
Maurice F. Strong
Julius Tahija
Russell E. Train
Charles A. Vaucher
Dr David P. S. Wasawo
Thomas J. Watson Jr

* *Members of the WWF Executive Council*

# WORLD WILDLIFE FUND ADDRESSES

*Headquarters*
World Wildlife Fund
CH-1110 Morges/Switzerland

*National Organizations*

**1. Austria**
Oesterreichischer
Stifterverband für
Naturschutz
angeschlossen dem
World Wildlife Fund
Festgasse 17, Postfach 1
1162 Vienna

**2. Belgium**
World Wildlife Fund Belgium
937 Ch. de Waterloo B5
1180 Bruxelles

**3. Canada**
World Wildlife Fund
60 St. Clair Av. East
Suite 201
Toronto M4T IN5/Ontario

**4. Denmark**
Verdensnaturfonden
(World Wildlife Fund Denmark)
Strandvejen 54
2900 Hellerup

**5. Finland**
Maailman Luonnon
Säätiö Suomen Rahasto
Hanuripolku 4
00420 Helsinki 42

**6. France**
Association Francaise
du World Wildlife Fund
23, rue d'Anjou
Paris 8e

**7. Germany**
Stiftung für die Gestaltung
und den Schutz der natürlichen
Umwelt
53 Bonn 12
Postfach 0363

**8. India**
World Wildlife Fund India
Great Western Building
S. Bhagat Singh Road
P.O. Box 1381
Bombay 400023

**9. Italy**
Associazione Italiana
per il World Wildlife Fund
Via P.A. Micheli 50
Rome 00197

**10. Japan**
World Wildlife Fund Japan
5F Yamaki Bldg.
Sotokanda 4-8-2
Chiyoda-ku
Tokyo 101

**11. Kenya**
World Wildlife Fund Kenya
P.O. Box 40075
Nairobi

**12. Luxembourg**
World Wildlife Fund Luxembourg
Musée d'Histoire Naturelle
Marché aux Poissons
Luxembourg

**13. Malaysia**
World Wildlife Fund Malaysia
8th floor Wisma Damansara
Jalan Semantan
P.O. Box 769
Kuala Lumpur

**14. Netherlands**
Wereld Natuur Fonds
Postbus 7
Zeist

**15. New Zealand**
World Wildlife Fund New Zealand
P.O. Box 12-200
North Wellington

**16. Norway**
World Wildlife Fund i Norge
Møllergt 24
Oslo 1

**17. Pakistan**
World Wildlife Fund Pakistan
P.O. Box 1312
Lahore

**18. Peru**
PRODENA—Pro Defensa de la Naturaleza
Pasaja Los Pinos 164/168
Edificio El Comodore
Alfredo Benavides
Lima

**19. South Africa**
The S.A. Nature Foundation
P.O. Box 456
Stellenbosch 7600

**20. Spain**
ADENA—Asociacion para la Defensa de la
Naturaleza
6, Joaquin Garcia Morato
Madrid-10

**21. Sweden**
Svenska Stiftelsen för World Wildlife Fund
Fituna
140 41 Sorunda
Stockholm Office:
Stureplan 3,
Stockholm

**22. Switzerland**
Stiftung World Wildlife Fund
Förrlibuckstr. 66
8037 Zurich

**23. Turkey**
Wildlife Foundation Turkey
Türkiye'de Dogayi Koruma Vakti
Büyükdere Caddesi 181 P.K. 126
Levent—Istanbul

**24. United Kingdom**
The World Wildlife Fund
29, Greville Street
London, EC1N 8AX

**25. United States**
World Wildlife Fund Inc.
1319 Eighteenth Street N.W.
Washington, D.C. 20036

**26. Venezuela**
FUDENA—Fundacion para la
Defensa de la Naturaleza
Apartado de Correo 70376
Caracas 107

# ACKNOWLEDGEMENTS

2–3 Erwin Bauer; 6 Philippa Scott; 13–14 William Oliver; 15 Christian Zuber/World Wildlife Fund; 16 J. C. Mallinson /WWF (top), William Oliver (centre), Christian Zuber/ WWF (bottom); 19 Keith Laidler; 21 Bruce Coleman/WWF (top left), Kenneth W. Green /WWF (bottom left), Keith Laidler (right); 23 Norman Myers/Bruce Coleman; 25 Ron Cartmell; 27 Simon Trevor/Bruce Coleman; 28–9 Hans Reinhard/Bruce Coleman; 30 Peter Johnson /NHPA; 31 Simon Trevor/Bruce Coleman; 32 Norman Myers/WWF; 33 Fievet/Jacana; 35 Bob Campbell/Bruce Coleman (top), Norman Myers/Bruce Coleman (bottom); 36 Norman Myers/Bruce Coleman; 37 Christian Zuber/Bruce Coleman; 39–44 Erich Hoyt; 49–51 David McKelvey; 53–61 Jeff Foott; 63–8 Anne LaBastille; 71–7 J. B. Nelson; 81 C. B. Frith/Bruce Coleman (top), Norman Myers/Bruce Coleman (bottom); 82–3 C. B. Frith/Bruce Coleman; 85 S. C. Bisserot/Bruce Coleman; 86 C. B. Frith/Bruce Coleman; 87 Natural History Photographic Agency (top), Norman Owen Tomalin/Bruce Coleman;  89 Willy Gamper; 91 W. Nägeli/WWF; 92–3 Robert Schulhof; 95–101 Leigh Plester; 103–9 Erwin Bauer; 111 Brian Hawkes/NHPA; 113 Heather Angel; 114 Bryan Sage; 115 G. Laycock/Bruce Coleman; 116 Bruce Coleman (top), M. F. Soper/Bruce Coleman (bottom); 117 Bryan Sage; 119 C. B. Frith/Bruce Coleman; 121 John A. Burton; 123–8 M. E. J. Gore; 131 C. A. W. Guggisberg/WWF; 132 I. Douglas-Hamilton/WWF; 135 Erwin Bauer; 137 Erich Hoyt

Paintings by John Barber

# INDEX

# Index